CW00663675

WORK ARISING

WORK ARISING

from the life

of

RUDOLF STEINER

*Articles published to mark
the fiftieth anniversary
of the death of Rudolf Steiner*

Edited by

JOHN DAVY

Rudolf Steiner Press

35 Park Road, London NW1 6XT

First printed 1975

© by J. Davy, A. C. Harwood, A. Klingborg, R. Raab, E. Hutchins, T. Weihs, L. F. Edmunds, M. R. Evans, H. H. Koepf, C. F. Budd, Nederlands Pedagogisch Instituut, O. L. Mathews and Rudolf Steiner Press, 1975

The illustrations of the Goetheanum buildings and the *Representative of Man* are published by permission of *Philosophisch Anthroposophischer Verlag* am Goetheanum, Switzerland.

ISBN 0 85440 293 4 (*cased edition*)
0 85440 294 2 (*paperback edition*)

MADE AND PRINTED IN GREAT BRITAIN BY
THE GARDEN CITY PRESS LIMITED
LETCHWORTH, HERTFORDSHIRE
SG6 1JS

CONTENTS

FOREWORD

Rudolf Steiner died on March 30th, 1925, in his studio workshop at Dornach, Switzerland. He lay beside a thirty-foot-high carving in wood of 'The Representative of Humanity' on which he had continued to work as long as he could.

The circumstances of his death show the central aim of his life: To open a way to a deeper understanding of man, and to translate this understanding into a renewal of human life and culture.

This collection of essays, which appears half a century later, is therefore not a memorial to the past, but a report on work in progress. Steiner died surrounded by new beginnings in many fields of work which he had helped to initiate. These have now developed and spread all over the world.

Two introductory essays offer some background to Steiner's life and thought; the remainder are contributed by people working in the fields they describe. The aim has been to report essentially on work which stands directly in everyday life, in the form of schools, farms, medical centres etcetera, and which embodies in one way or another a new social impulse. Much has been omitted, notably a more detailed survey of current work in some of the arts and sciences, but an appendix gives sources of further information.

Above all, I hope that these essays will convey something of the experience of those now working out of Steiner's

Anthroposophy (very few of whom ever knew Steiner himself), which is that the ways he opened up become more fruitful, rewarding and relevant to the urgent needs of our times with every year that passes.

JOHN DAVY

1. RUDOLF STEINER

Initiate of the Will

by JOHN DAVY

This book is about a renewal of work in many spheres of human life—a renewal which has its origins in the life and work of Rudolf Steiner, who died on March 30th, 1925.

Moving around the world today, you may come across a school, a farm, a village community for mentally handicapped adults, a group of doctors running a hospital, a group of architects, a scientific laboratory, artists, drama groups, a substantial pharmaceutical firm, a toy factory, an industrial consultancy, a bank, and other enterprises, all of them acknowledging a fundamental debt to Steiner.

This debt is centred in a view of the human being and the significance of his life on earth to which Steiner gave the name 'Anthroposophy'. But it is a view which has led right into the details of work in many different professions.

It is easy to recognise that one man may inspire many others with some kind of common philosophical or moral outlook. It is harder to accept that he could have sufficient expertise in so many different fields that he could offer detailed practical help in all of them. Yet this was the actual experience of those who asked Steiner, during his lifetime, for help in renewing many kinds of work, and it continues to be the experience of those who have followed on.

But the most formidable obstacle for the modern mind is

9

to comprehend Steiner as an 'Initiate'—as a human being possessing capacities of spiritual perception developed to a very high degree. The aim of this chapter is to sketch Steiner's own life so as to throw light on the questions this raises. What was Steiner himself attempting to do? How was it possible for him to give detailed and fruitful help in such diverse fields of work and knowledge? What kind of a man was he, and what is the nature of the world-wide anthroposophical movement to which his life has given rise?

*　　*　　*

The word 'Initiate' has for modern ears uncomfortable connotations of privileged access to some mysterious body of knowledge. It was properly so understood in earlier times when whole cultures were guided, from temples and mystery centres, by priests or priest-kings. The Initiates, in one form or another, were an elite, inspired by their gods to guide their peoples. Something of this still echoes on in the spiritual authority often claimed today by Eastern gurus, and granted to them by their pupils and followers.

To see Steiner as an Austrian spiritual teacher in this sense is completely to misunderstand his position (which is not to say that he did not have to combat throughout his life attempts by some followers to make him one). We come closer by recognising that the word 'initiate' can also be a verb, meaning quite simply to start something new.

The human capacity to start something new, to invent, to create, is the unique feature of our nature which distinguishes us most clearly from animals (even the most advanced performances of some higher apes are rudimentary compared with our own). It is a faculty both mysterious and very highly prized in our culture. We are not prepared, nowadays, to leave creative initiative to a few gurus or leaders, but claim, at the very least, the right of every one to formulate his own thoughts, coloured by his own feelings, and to translate these, in so far as they can be absorbed by the community, into actions. Steiner belongs explicitly within this essentially Western tradition of individual spiritual freedom in judgement and striving.

It is a matter of common experience that the ultimate sources of our creative faculties are unconscious. We cannot say where a good idea 'comes from', or what determines its emergence into our waking consciousness at a given moment. Various schools of psychoanalysis have indicated possibilities of looking more deeply into the unconscious. Steiner regarded these explorations as limited and confused, through being undertaken with quite inadequate powers of cognition. He was concerned, therefore, to show a 'path of knowledge' whereby, in the words which open his book *Knowledge of the Higher Worlds*, 'faculties which slumber in every human being' may be gradually discovered and developed. His position is democratic rather than aristocratic, showing a way to his fellows rather than teaching a privileged revelation to followers. He may perhaps be described, therefore, as an Initiate of the will (in contrast to the Initiates of wisdom of former times).

The path he described, leading right into the practical tasks of modern life, was one he had lived and struggled with himself during the first forty years of his life, although he spoke very little about his own experiences until the last year or so before he died, when he set down a very sober account in an uncompleted autobiography.* This was written partly in response to the urging of friends who wanted him to set the record straight, at a time when opponents in central Europe, during the early 1920s, were circulating a variety of scurrilous attacks on him and his work. Only a few themes from this account can be highlighted here.

Steiner's first forty years brought a remarkable diversity

* Rudolf Steiner, *The Course of My Life* (Anthroposophic Press Inc., New York, 1951)

of experience. He was born on February 27th, 1861 in a tiny rural village, Kraljevec, in Upper Austria, surrounded by an agricultural, social and religious way of life with its roots deep in the past. At the same time, the modern age was knocking at the door, in the form of the railway and the telegraph, which was served by Steiner's father, a station-master. The family soon moved, first to Mödling and then to Pottschach in Lower Austria near the Alps. When Steiner was eight, there came another move to Neudörfl near Wiener Neustadt. The mountains were more distant, and the city of Vienna was coming closer.

He attended the village schools, but learned most from listening to the peasants, and to the talk of the doctor, the priest and the mayor when they gathered at the station (which was a kind of social centre), from watching his father at work and exploring the local flour mill.

Throughout this period, he was full of questions, and rather lonely. A major cause of this loneliness was his early discovery that his inner life brought him, as a matter of course, perceptions and experiences that were not shared by the adults around him. Steiner is reticent about the details of these experiences, saying simply that 'the reality of the spiritual world was to me as certain as that of the physical', and that by the age of eight he had learned to distinguish between things and beings which are 'seen' and those which are 'not seen'. It seems, though, that he would become aware of individuals who had died—for example, he found himself approached, with a kind of request for help, by a woman who had committed suicide in the village an hour or two earlier. He would also be aware of elemental beings at work in nature.

Such experiences are probably more common among young children than is often realised, and are usually dis-missed by sceptical adults as fantasy. Many children must have shared a similar loneliness to Steiner's. But it does seem that this gift of inner vision was quite unusually full and clear in Steiner's case, and did not fade as he grew up. (Wordsworth, by contrast, remembered clearly the 'shades of the prison house' closing on his boyhood.)

The problem of the 'seen' and 'unseen' worlds created for Steiner a burning question which became a dominant theme of his first thirty years. He describes how a first glimpse of a way forward came to him from an unexpected source when he picked up a geometry book in the room of the assistant teacher at Neudörfl. Here was a remarkable phenomenon—a book about 'unseen' realities which was yet publicly accepted knowledge. 'I learned through geometry', Steiner writes, 'to know happiness for the first time.' We shall return to the significance of this later. But it would be a mistake to picture a withdrawn and dreamy child, precociously preoccupied with geometry in a small village school. For despite this intense and private inward life, he took a full part in the life around him—not least in the chores of a poor home, fetching wood and water, gathering berries in the woods, raising vegetables etcetera.

A normal course for a gifted village pupil at that time would have been to go on to grammar school and then to a seminary. But Steiner's father was a freethinker, and in any case saw his son as a railway engineer rather than a priest. So the boy was sent to the 'modern' school in Wiener Neustadt where the emphasis was on sciences. Here he did well, although in some classes, notably history, he was inattentive for two reasons: he discovered that the history teacher was simply expounding from a textbook which he could more conveniently absorb at home; and he had discovered the works of Emmanuel Kant. Steiner therefore bound Kant into the covers of his history textbook, and read the *Critique of Pure Reason* while apparently following attentively the teacher's exposition.

What could Kant mean to a fifteen-year-old? Steiner had

discovered someone struggling with his own problem of the seen and the unseen, but from an opposite point of view. Where Steiner was searching intensely for a bridge between spiritual reality and human knowledge, Kant was making an absolute gulf—a gulf which was deepening the separation of faith and reason.

The 'prison house' for human thinking, experienced so vividly by Wordsworth, was cemented by Kant into a declaration that we can never know the 'things in themselves' of nature, but only our own pictures of things. But for Steiner, there existed within man 'a sort of soul space which is the scene of action of spiritual beings and occurrences. I could not look upon thoughts as something like images which the human beings form of things; on the contrary, I saw in them revelations of a spiritual world on this field of action in the soul.'*

From Wiener Neustadt, Steiner went on to the Technical High School in Vienna to study mathematics, natural history and chemistry. Almost immediately he had two important encounters. The first was with an old peasant herb gatherer who travelled on the same train into the city. This man had no formal education, but possessed faculties of spiritual perception which allowed him to see deep into the secrets of nature and know, for example, the curative properties of the herbs he gathered. Through this friendship, Steiner realised he was meeting a last representative of an instinctive clairvoyance of an earlier era. The old man had developed his own strange language for describing his perceptions, but Steiner soon learned to understand him, and the relationship meant a great deal to the young student. The peasant appeared later as a character in Steiner's Mystery Plays, Felix Balde.

The other encounter was with Professor Karl Julius Schroer, the great Goethe scholar who came regularly to

* Op. cit., Ch. 1

lecture on German literature at the Technical High School. They became friends, and Schroer encouraged Steiner to make a deeper study of Goethe. This led to an invitation to write introductions to Goethe's scientific works for the new Kürschner edition. In these works, Steiner found an approach to nature closely linked with his own, for he was by this time deeply concerned to relate his spiritual perceptions to the findings of natural science. He later referred frequently to Goethe's work as containing seeds for the future of science—and particularly for the science of the living world—of the utmost importance. This work is still little known or understood, and this is not the place to review it in any detail, but it led Goethe, for example, to perceive within all the varying forms of the plant world manifestations of one *Ur-Pflanze* or Archetypal Plant, present not as an abstract thought or Idea, but as a living creative spiritual reality in all plants.

Throughout his twenties, Steiner studied widely and deeply in the philosophy and science of his time in his struggle to relate his spiritual perception with the culture around him, and by 1890, he was beginning to find clarity. This phase of his life came to fruition, first in a doctoral thesis (published in 1892 as *Wahrheit und Wissenschaft*),* and then in *Die Philosophie der Freiheit*† (first published in 1894). The latter he described in a letter to a friend as a kind of 'biography of a soul striving upwards towards freedom'. In this book, Steiner shows how in the activity of thinking we do not simply make pictures of some other and forever unknowable reality, but participate in reality itself, both in knowing and in creative action. The thread of the argument cannot be traced here, but for Steiner himself, the

* In English, *Truth and Science*, published in the same volume as *The Philosophy of Spiritual Activity* (Rudolf Steiner Publications Inc., New York, 1963)

† *The Philosophy of Spiritual Activity*, as above, or with the title *The Philosophy of Freedom* (Rudolf Steiner Press, London, 1964)

book brought a certain resolution of the dilemma which had been with him from early childhood. There is nothing specific in *The Philosophy of Freedom* about spiritual perception or experience (apart from some footnotes added in a later edition), but its implication is clear: there are no absolute limits to knowledge of the kind posited by Kant, but only limitations of individual capacity and experience. A path of development lies open from the normal capacities of thought and feeling possessed by every man to the modes of apprehension open to Steiner since childhood. Our modern intellect may be a kind of prison house, but the door is not locked. And we can leave without escaping into obscure mysticism or leaving behind the clarity and certainty we have won through a modern scientific consciousness.

During this period (starting already while at school in Wiener Neustadt) Steiner supported himself mainly by tutoring. Perhaps the most remarkable episode in this connection was his work with a Vienna family of four children, one of whom was backward with a hydrocephalic condition. Steiner found ways of working with him which rapidly improved this condition, and made it possible for the boy to enter grammar school and eventually to qualify as a doctor. Steiner also tutored fellow students and adults, mainly in mathematics and natural science. These tutoring experiences no doubt bore fruit much later when he began to work for a renewal in education of both normal and handicapped children.

A further dimension of Steiner's student life in Vienna was his activity in the 'Reading Hall' of the Technical High School—a kind of students' union—where he first became librarian and then president. He kept free of any political commitment, but observed political life both among the students, and from the gallery in the Austrian Parliament. Much that later broke out during and after the First World War could there, Steiner wrote, be experienced in germ.

After graduating, and while working as a tutor in Vienna, Steiner also came to know a wide circle of artists, poets and intellectuals in Vienna, including the radical but pessimistic circle round Marie Eugenie delle Grazie, whose heroes were Dostoievski and Leopold von Sacher-Masoch. Their beliefs were directly opposed to the Idealism of Schroer, a contrast which Steiner found both painful and stimulating.

He also held for a brief period the editorship of a literary and political journal, the *Deutsche Wochenschrift*, and had to write weekly on current social and political questions. Through this post, he came to know, in particular, some of the leaders of the Socialist movement in Austria at that time, and to study Marx, Engels and other left-wing writers. Steiner began to be deeply concerned with the social questions of his time, but was convinced that no adequate progress could be made without understanding the spiritual nature of the human being. At the same time as Steiner's inner struggle with the problem of knowledge was coming to fruition, there were taking shape for him burning questions which were to preoccupy him during his thirties, and bear fruit much later in the impulses for social renewal and work in many practical fields towards the end of his life. These questions had to do, in a certain way, with the problem of finding the reality of the spirit not only within his own soul, but in the surrounding world—and learning to meet, at the same time, enormous forces of opposition.

In the autumn of 1890, Steiner moved to Weimar in Germany, where he worked for the next seven years in the Goethe archives, responsible particularly for preparing a complete edition of Goethe's scientific works, but also bringing out collections of work by other authors, including a complete edition of Schopenhauer. The place was also a major cultural centre, with a theatre and concerts, and was visited by leading lights of Central Europe's cultural life all round the year. Here Steiner's active literary and social life became ever fuller and broader, while his inner life began to approach a new crisis.

This was connected with an awakening of a capacity for much clearer and more precise observation of the world around him. In this respect, Steiner says of himself, he was developing rather late capacities which awaken naturally in most people in quite early childhood. But right up into his thirties, while he had been able to grasp concepts and their connections with ease, he had experienced great difficulty in retaining clear and detailed impressions acquired through the senses. Now all this changed—and led to a deepening of his spiritual perceptions as well. In describing this change, Steiner mentions two significant things: he had long had a regular practice of meditation, out of a recognition of its value for the spiritual life; now, though, meditation became a *necessity*. At the same time, he says, 'the idea-element in the preceding life retired in a certain aspect and the will-element took its place'.*

One can picture this change in Steiner's life by comparing it to an everyday experience, when a person moves from contemplation to action—when an idea, for example, which brought understanding, begins to be translated into an ideal for action. Then new energies well up, but at the same time, as soon as an idea is spoken out, something irrevocable has happened. The speaker is vulnerable to opposition in a way in which the contemplative listener is not. He has to stand in the world for his idea.

As the years at Weimar passed, Steiner began to face with growing intensity the inner question, 'Must I stay silent?' He had entered deeply into many forms of culture around him, and his own contributions had been clothed in language and forms of thought in which nothing direct was

* Op. cit., Ch. 22, p. 246

said about perception of spiritual beings or spiritual worlds. Now he began to feel a growing need and urgency to speak out more directly, not only for his own sake, but in response to the urgent needs of the times. But in facing this prospect, he had also to face inwardly, as spiritual reality, those forces which would imprison humanity permanently in a 'prison-house' consciousness, aware only of material entities and mechanical processes.

As this struggle was coming to a head, Steiner left Weimar for Berlin, where he became editor of an avante-garde literary magazine, and found himself associating with the German equivalent of what would now be called the radical left, or even the underground. As well as writing, he co-produced, with Otto Hartleben, a number of modern plays for the Free Dramatic Society associated with the magazine.

Soon after arriving in Berlin, he was also approached by the directors of the Berlin Worker's Training School, sponsored by the trade unions and social democrats. The teaching in this school was almost exclusively Marxist-Leninist, but Steiner insisted on, and got, a free hand. He gave courses on history and natural science, and practical exercises in public speaking. His appeal to the trade unionists was such that he was invited to give a festival address to seven thousand type-setters and printers in the Berlin circus stadium on the occasion of the Gutenberg jubilee. His refusal to commit himself to a defined party position, though, did not endear him to some of the political activists in union circles, and soon after the turn of the century he was forced to drop this work.

In their different ways, both the workers and the artistic bourgeoisie with whom Steiner was associated at this time were searching for a new age, for new freedoms within and a new social order without. It was during this time that Steiner's inner life led him to contemplate the spiritual meaning of Christianity. He had written at times some sharp criticisms of doctrinal and organised Christianity, but now he came to perceive inwardly what the Incarnation signified for the life of the earth and for all men. He perceived it as a spiritual turning point for all humanity, planting within the earth and man a creative source which could grow towards individual freedom and love. This perception was a turning point for Steiner himself, a culmination of his own path of initiation, and determined the remaining years of his life. During these years, he learned to speak out, with growing directness, of the spiritual realities within which we live, of the evolution of man and the urgent needs of the present times, yet never in obscure or didactic language, appealing always to the ordinary healthy intelligence of those who wished to listen.

At first he found these mainly among members of the Theosophical movement, within which he worked at first as an independent lecturer and teacher. Until about 1909, most of his work was in the form of lectures, talks and articles, gradually formulating a 'spiritual science', and travelling all over Europe. He soon met a remarkable and dynamic actress and artist, Marie von Sivers, of Russian extraction, who later became his wife. Gradually they began to imbue this activity of exposition and teaching with artistic elements—particularly dramatic recitations.

At the same time, Steiner found himself increasingly at odds with some aspects of the Theosophical movement, notably their rejection of science and their heavy emphasis on Eastern spiritual teachings and practices. This came to a head when a young Indian boy was proclaimed the chosen vessel for a new incarnation of Christ. Steiner refused to go along with this absurdity, and in 1913 was excluded from the Theosophical Society. This led to the founding of an independent Anthroposophical Society in the same year.

Four years earlier, Steiner had begun to write a series of remarkable Mystery Plays, and to produce them in Munich with Marie von Sivers. The hope was to build a permanent home for such work in the city. Problems with the city planners, and an offer of land in Switzerland, led to plans for the first 'Goetheanum' on a hill above Dornach near Basle. The foundation stone was laid shortly before the outbreak of the First World War. Throughout the years that followed, a mixed group of craftsmen and amateurs from many nations worked together to raise the two interlocking domes and carve the rows of great wooden pillars to create what Steiner said was to be a 'House of Speech'. Here speech and drama were nurtured, eurythmy—a new art of movement—was developed; painters created under Steiner's guidance vast murals on the domes. It was a true workshop of the arts, and marked a further stage in Steiner's efforts to place something embodying spiritual truths into the life of the times.

Finally, from 1917 onwards, as the war was clearly nearing its end, a final phase of Steiner's life opened, some of the fruits of which are described in this book, so that only a brief glimpse is needed here. In the post-war chaos of Europe, many were seeking new beginnings for social life and work—and growing numbers of people began to approach Steiner for help. In 1919, a Stuttgart industrialist, Emil Molt, asked Steiner to help him open a new school for the children of the employees in his cigarette factory. Thus the first Waldorf school was born. Scientists, doctors, farmers, theologians came too—and prompted Steiner to a series of remarkable lecture courses, together with much practical guidance and advice. Steiner also saw an opportunity for developing a deeper understanding of social, political and economic life, and even trying to put something into practice. Out of this came a series of books and lectures on the 'threefold social order'. This is not a recipe or a political programme, but a description of social functions present in every modern society, which reflect corresponding functions in man himself. The task, Steiner held, is to recognise these functions more clearly (which are as distinct in their requirements and laws as the nervous system is from the digestive system in man), and to provide more consciously for a healthy cultural, legislative and economic life.

Here Steiner was drawn into a heavy programme of writing and lecturing, and became a well-known and highly controversial figure in post-war Germany—so much so that his life was threatened by extremists of several kinds. On New Year's night 1922, an arsonist set fire to the Goetheanum, which burned to the ground.

Undaunted, Steiner set to work and designed a second building, constructed in concrete, which still stands. A new foundation ceremony was held at Christmas 1923, and this ushered in nine months of intensely creative work which still nourishes in a quite remarkable way the anthroposophical activities which have grown up in the past half century.

At Michaelmas 1924, Steiner's strength gave out, and he fell ill. He continued writing from his sickbed—including the chapters of his autobiography—until he died on March 30th, 1925. When one surveys this whole life, one is impressed at first by the rich variety of experience: the peasant villages of Austria, the intellectual and cultural life of Vienna and Weimar; the radicals and the working men of Berlin; the erudition, lightly worn, of a human being of immense and unflagging energies who had contrived to immerse himself deeply in philosophy, literature, science, the arts and politics of his time with a universality rare in an age of specialisation.

*   *   *

Standing back from this, and trying to grasp Steiner's inner path, there emerges a remarkable picture of the metamorphosis of a personal inner struggle into a public work for a truly human society, in the course of which Steiner had to face ostracism from many old friends and acquaintances from the moment he began to speak openly of spiritual realities in man and the world. This uncomfortable directness which informs Steiner's anthroposophical work, together with its sobriety, disconcerts many who come across it. He cannot be placed in any familiar slot, and the result is a remarkable blank—which anthroposophists may be forgiven for seeing at times almost as a conspiracy of silence—in public awareness of Steiner and his work.

It is no accident that some of the last and most significant of Steiner's lecture courses were concerned with reincarnation and destiny, and their bearing on human history and individual biography. He described there the deep unconscious forces in the human will that guide a person to meet crucial experiences of life, and how, in each encounter with the metamorphosed consequences of a previous life, there open free opportunities for creative initiative into the future. To perceive clearly the realities of human destiny, Steiner said, belongs to the most demanding and difficult tasks of 'spiritual research'. Yet out of individual destinies, the fabric of social life is woven. It is likely to be some time before awareness of these realities becomes part of life for the majority—although one can scarcely imagine a more far-reaching realisation for both individual life and social life as a whole.

This was the final, and perhaps most crucial, part of Steiner's own destiny, so that he departed surrounded by beginnings. That the seeds he left were fertile, the past fifty years have shown. This book is offered in the conviction that although the seeds have germinated, the main growth is still to come.

FURTHER READING

Rudolf Steiner, *The Course of My Life* (Anthroposophic Press Inc., N.Y., 1951)

Rudolf Steiner, *Knowledge of the Higher Worlds. How is it achieved?* (Rudolf Steiner Press, London, 1969)

Rudolf Steiner, *The Philosophy of Freedom* (Rudolf Steiner Press, London, 1964)

2. THREEFOLD MAN

Rudolf Steiner's Key to Social Renewal

by CECIL HARWOOD

Rudolf Steiner made it his first task to awaken a generation caught in the confines of sense-perception to the possibility of perceiving other worlds and other Beings than those that manifest themselves to the senses. The poets and mystics have always spoken of such worlds.

> O World invisible, we view thee,
> O World intangible, we touch thee,
> O World unknowable, we know thee,
> Inapprehensible, we clutch thee.

Their object however was to stir the depths of the feeling heart, his, to rear an edifice of spiritual knowledge equal in accuracy to, but wider in scope than, natural science, a knowledge based not on the intellect alone but on the full gamut of human faculties. This edifice embraced universe, earth and man. It contained, indeed, not a little ancient knowledge jettisoned by the science of the modern age, but given fresh form and new significance. It is therefore fundamentally a new knowledge, new in conception, new in presentation, new in the demands it makes on those who seek to understand it. It is a knowledge which, at its name. Anthroposophy implies, regards man not as a peripheral accident, but as central to the understanding of the entire universe.

Forces invisible and intangible are fully recognised by natural science when they manifest themselves in the visible, tangible, physical world. Electricity is invisible, gravity is invisible. Indeed Newton was accused by French philosophers of re-introducing magic into the universe in making a force acting at a distance one of its primary constituents. But such invisible forces are accepted only if they can be expressed mathematically, whereas Steiner pointed out that there is equal evidence for a world of formative forces, manifesting in the plant kingdom artistically rather than mathematically.

He called this world, visible to the clairvoyant, by a traditional name—the world of the etheric forces. The animal kingdom adds to these etheric forces a world of sentience, for which again he used the traditional name of astral forces, also visible to the clairvoyant. The human being adds to these physical, etheric and astral worlds a fourth principle which indeed raises the other three into a new dimension and gives them new functions. It is the principle of the ego by virtue of which every man calls himself 'I', combines his experiences of life into a unique biography through the power of memory, lives in a world of ideas as well as sense-perceptions, develops art, science, philosophy, religion.

In the earlier years of his teaching about man, Steiner was principally concerned with developing the picture of this 'fourfold man', describing, for instance, the genesis of the four principles in the evolution of the earth. He was still concerned with a cosmogony and was not yet involved in any practical application of his ideas. Thus, for instance, his first little book on Education* is entirely based on the fourfold man, and the successive manifestation of the four principles in the stages of childhood and youth.

* *The Education of the Child in the Light of Anthroposophy* (1909) (Rudolf Steiner Press, London, 1965)

26

It was not till after the First World War that a variety of people came to him and asked his help in establishing practical work in many fields of activity based on his ideas and ideals. Between that time and the earlier period in which he was developing a cosmogony, better called an anthroposophy, Steiner had done much creative work in the arts. This included the writing and production of four Mystery Plays, the creation of a new art of movement called Eurythmy, and the building of an immense auditorium and stage in a completely original style of architecture. But during all this time he had been elaborating a new conception of man not as a fourfold but as a threefold being. He had actually worked on the idea for thirty years before making it publicly known in 1919. He subsequently described this view of man as a threefold being as making it possible for modern man to realise in a new form the old Greek Mystery precept: Man, know thyself. It was largely on this view of man that practical activities could be, and were, founded.

Steiner's philosophy had always been Trinitarian: he spoke in terms of Body, Soul and Spirit, when the prevailing view of man was—and indeed still is—dualistic, Body and Mind, if not monistic, Body alone. In psychology also he postulated three fundamental powers of the soul: thinking, feeling and willing, each with its different kind and degree of consciousness, and none of them ever appearing in pure isolation. That thinking is more related to the Spirit, feeling to the Soul, and willing to the Body was more or less self evident. But he had not as yet related them to systems within the physical body. He had indeed described different processes or systems in the physical body as being severally and specially related to the four 'principles'. But Steiner now revealed an over-mastering picture of a threefold organisation which related equally to Body, Soul and Spirit. And whereas a knowledge of the principles can be traced back to Eastern tradition and Greek philosophy, the conception of the threefold organisation of man is entirely new in the history of human thought. In the process of history the youngest principle—the ego—has penetrated the depths of the physical body, in doing which it has found a new definition but has lost its cosmic relationship. This can only be fully recovered again when body, soul and spirit are realised as a unity through the conception of threefold man.

For the Greeks, said Steiner, the ego had not shrunk to its present abstract point; they could instinctively apprehend the worlds of Spirit, Soul and Body and had a true sense of Man in his fulness when they uttered the ancient Sun-word of Apollo, Know thyself. We today must consciously add: Know thyself in Spirit, Soul and Body.

In an age when all experience is treated in many influential schools of thought as purely somatic, perhaps the first thing to note is that Steiner made an absolute distinction between the experience of the physical senses and that of the soul, and between these two and that of the spirit. The three may indeed be received simultaneously—and in modern consciousness generally are—but this does not mean that they are identical. The pleasure I receive from a landscape or picture is not a matter of sense-perception. It is an experience of the soul, of the world of feeling. But I would not be able to have pleasure in a landscape or picture unless I could first of all recognise it as such. This recognition goes beyond the world of pleasure or feeling, just as the pleasure or feeling goes beyond the mere sense perception. It depends on a world of the mind informing the world given by the senses, which would otherwise be a disconnected sequence or jumble of sense impressions. The world of the mind is the beginning of what Steiner calls the world of spirit. If this world of the mind were purely subjective and peculiar to me I would of course be unable to make any bridge to your, or anyone's, world of the mind, and we would all live our lives in isolation. Happily this is not so, except in cases of extreme aberration. Contrary to what most people imagine, the world of sense perceptions is a private world, conditioned by our individual standpoint, while the world of ideas is a public world in which, stripped of personal accretions, we all share alike. Mathematics, where we suffer least from these personal accretions, shows us most clearly this common or public nature of the world of ideas. Your idea of a triangle is numerically identical with mine—yours cannot contain less, nor mine more, than two right angles. Your pleasure in, or dislike of, mathematics may be greater than mine—*de gustibus non est disputandum*—but we both recognise its validity as a system of thought not dependent on our personal experience of life. Actually it is this valid world of ideas which makes all our thinking even about the sense world possible. In our age, however, our attention has become so concentrated on the sense world that we even deny the existence of an independent world of the mind. It is, however, the starting point of Anthroposophy as against the Natural Scientific view of the world, which begins with the senses. For Anthroposophy regards the abstract thought of modern science not as the highest manifestation of a somatic process, but as the lowest manifestation of a world of living ideas. It aims at perfecting not so much the external instruments which enlarge the field of sense perception, as the cognitional organs of the thinker himself, so that he may enter the world where thoughts are not abstract or lifeless, but living and active—and that, for Steiner, is the world of Spirit. It is because this world of Spirit informs also the physical world, as well as man himself, that in contemplating that world man is able to illuminate it with the light of a consciousness that goes beyond mere sense perception and beyond the realm of feeling.

Out of such considerations as these there arises again in a new way the threefold nature of man as consisting of Body, Soul and Spirit, which Steiner had advanced from the beginning of his work. But now it appears in such a way that each of these three entities is considered as possessing in itself a threefold nature which is reflected in the other two and binds all three together as a unity.

The central entity is that of the psyche or soul, which is seen as drawing its experience both from the physical side of man's nature, and from the spiritual. It is the best starting point for a description of threefold man.

The three fundamental powers of the human soul, thought, feeling and will, never appear in complete isolation from each other; but (as Coleridge observed) we must learn to distinguish even when we cannot divide.

We can distinguish them in many ways. In thinking, essentially considered, we enjoy the clearest consciousness. Indeed no true thinking takes place unless our ego is active in the process. Day dreaming proceeds of its own accord with a minimal amount of consciousness. Thinking is one pole of the soul's activities. At the opposite pole is willing, of which we are almost totally unconscious—when we move an arm or a leg we do not know how our will takes hold of the muscle which effects the movement. It is really a magical process, the direct action of consciousness on matter. But between the polar opposites of thinking and will there is a middle term, a mean, namely the life of feeling, which is neither as conscious as thinking, nor as unconscious as will. If in thinking we are awake and in willing we are asleep, it may be said that in feeling we dream.

We can also distinguish the three from the standpoint of time. Our thinking enters us from the past. We inevitably think of the future in terms of the past—that is why we have so few prophets. All our will actions carry us into the future. We live most deeply in the present through the operation of feeling, in which we can become so absorbed that time almost ceases to exist.

What is the physical basis of these three powers of the

soul? Steiner had a unique and revolutionary answer to this question. As against the Cartesian view that all consciousness is based on the brain and nerves, while the rest of the body performs organic functions only (a view never held before the time of Descartes), Steiner held that the whole body is the vehicle of the soul. He began by accepting the finding of natural science that the intellectual thinking of today is based on the brain and nervous system, but he held that this is true only of modern intellectual thought. This is already a reservation, but there are also other important differences. Natural science still—for the most part—speaks of certain nerves, motor nerves, as carrying the impulses of will. Steiner did not accept this view, but held that the nerves provided that minimal amount of consciousness which made the operation of the will possible.* His view of the sense organs was also revolutionary, as he held that eye, ear etcetera are not essentially inner organs of the body, but are creations by forces of the outer world 'inserted' into the physical body itself, so that the psyche meets the actual world in the sense organ and not mere vibrations etcetera issuing from that world. He also rejected the idea that consciousness is a kind of metabolism of the nerves or brain, pointing out that there is a minimal amount of metabolism in those organs, which may rather be said to contain a continual process of destruction. It is this death process, this suppression of life, which enables individual consciousness to penetrate and find its support in the physical body. It is when the living Spirit, the World Life, has no creative physical work to perform that the brain can act as a mirror, and thought can become fully conscious.

Just as, psychologically considered, the will is the polar opposite process to conscious thinking, so the bodily system

* Something of this view is already entering Natural Science. See the paper by Dr. J. A. V. Bates in *Lectures on the Scientific Basis of Medicine*, vol. 5, 1955–6

through which it functions is polarically opposite to the system of head and nerves. This is the metabolic system, with which Steiner associated the system of the limbs, of free movement. The relation between will and metabolism, which is a process of life, must necessarily be very different from that between consciousness and the head and nerves, a system devoid of life, in which there are 'no moving parts'. The former relation cannot be localised, as can the latter. It is a relation of function and process rather than of demonstrable physical correspondences. That this latter relationship was universally assumed in earlier ages is demonstrated by such surviving phrases as 'bowels of compassion', 'lily livered', 'having no stomach for the fight'. If ideation and consciousness are carried to all parts of the body through the nerves, the will impulse is so carried by the blood. The relation of will with the limb system can also become a matter of experience. 'Putting a foot down' is not a mere metaphor. Even today many people can feel how a resolution of the will calls for a stiffening of the limbs, a clenching of the jaws (which represent the limbs in the sphere of the head). Shakespeare's Henry V summons up the courage of his troops by calling on them to 'stiffen the sinews, summon up the blood'—the blood which carries the will impulse through the body as the nerves carry consciousness.

In between thinking and willing lies the great intermediary, feeling. There is no true way from thinking to action except through feeling. We all know how easy it is to perform some action to which we are sympathetic, how difficult one to which we have an antipathy, how we actually even forget the thing we proposed to do in the latter but never in the former case. The greatest of all feelings, Love, has always been associated in popular belief with the human heart, but it needed a Steiner to assert and to enlarge that belief as a scientific fact.

In respect of consciousness we have found feeling an

32

• •

intermediary between thinking and will, not so conscious as
the one and more conscious than the other. Correspondingly,
the physical basis of feeling is the rhythmic organisation, the
chest system, lying between the stillness of the head and the
varying movement of the metabolism and voluntary movement of the limbs. The rhythmic movement of breathing and
blood circulation, heart and lungs, may be said to combine
the qualities both of stillness and movement, for its movement is one which never ceases and never tires. The muscles
of heart and lungs never grow weary from the first inbreath
of life to the expiry of death. When rhythm is brought into
voluntary movement it at once increases strength and miti-
gates fatigue. In an age when the human body was the
principle source of energy this was well understood. There
were spinning songs, milking songs, songs for churning
butter, songs for hauling logs. Soldiers sang as they marched,
sailors sang their sea-chanties at the capstan, the errand boy
whistled in the city streets. And if rhythm affects the will,
everyone knows that feeling affects the rhythmic system. The
heart beats high with hope—we catch our breath in surprise.

Thus we have three systems of the body which act in their
different ways as the basis of the three soul powers. But just
as thinking, feeling and will are always intermingled, so the
three bodily systems interpenetrate each other, and each of
them works within the fields of the other two. In modern
anatomy the various organs can be separated by dissection.
The three systems of threefold man, like the three soul
powers, may be distinguished but they cannot be divided.
Intellectual thinking can divide. It requires imaginative
thinking to distinguish.

There is so much evidence available in actual experience
for the relation of the three soul powers with the three
bodily systems that their connection is not difficult to grasp.
More difficult to comprehend is their relation to the three
spiritual powers, which, taken together, have been called the

'noetically real'.* The whole of Steiner's Anthroposophy, however, depends on the fact that this 'noetically real' is a threefold entity, which can—and does—inform the psyche and work into the bodily principles in a threefold way. The modern scientific outlook in general holds the view that the spiritual—if it believes in it at all—manifests itself in thinking alone, and is essentially the highest manifestation of purely organic processes. For Steiner, however, modern intellectual thinking is the lowest manifestation of Spirit. It does indeed have its roots in the Spirit but, in order to become individual consciousness, it kills the living element of Spirit, and confines itself to those reflections which we call abstract ideas. On the other hand that same Spirit enters fully with its magical creative powers into the system of limbs and metabolism, where there is almost no individual consciousness, and into the rhythmic system where consciousness and life processes live in the equilibrium of a dream.

For thinking to become alive it must free itself from the brain, and attain direct access to the living world of Spirit. In Steiner's spiritual terminology, which has no equivalent in ordinary psychology, this means to attain the stage of Imagination, towards which imagination in its common meaning may be considered as a kind of instinctive first step. Steiner has frequently described specific exercises by which it may be attained.† He describes it as having fundamentally a pictorial character, and stresses the danger it brings of falling into illusion.

Spirit enters the life of feeling from two directions, from the conscious thinking of the head and from the unconsciousness of the will in the limbs and metabolism. To bring the two consciously together means not only to enliven and deepen the consciousness but to awaken the element of will. It is in the rhythmic system, reaching the head system more

* Cf. *The Case for Anthroposophy* (Rudolf Steiner Press, London, 1970)
† Cf. *Occult Science—An Outline*, Ch. V

through breath, and the will system more through the blood, that such a union may be attained. We speak of moments of 'inspiration' where we draw on a world of living spirit not ordinarily attainable, and such moments may be regarded as a flashing into consciousness of something from a world even deeper than imagination. To live consciously and voluntarily in this world is to attain what Steiner calls the state of Inspiration. A third, and still deeper consciousness, is attained when we penetrate even the will with consciousness and feeling. It is the state which occasionally stirs into conscious life when we say we have an 'intuition.' To live consciously and voluntarily in this world—a very different matter—is to achieve the state which Steiner calls Intuition. Actually we are guided by our unconscious intuitions far more than we realise. When an older man looks back on the form of his life he realises how little he has really directed it, and how much it has arisen from will impulses of which he never foresaw the results. The spiritual direction of our life— our karma—proceeds from our unconscious will.

If we raise our consciousness to Imagination we begin to perceive living pictures of the spiritual world. Inspiration wakens in us the experience of that world which was ours before our birth. Intuition brings into our consciousness our previous earth life, which conditions our karma in the present life. Thus we have continually flowing into both soul and body forces from the world of Spirit, of which there was once an instinctive apprehension, but of which we are no longer aware since Descartes and his school of thought imprisoned us in the intellect. 'I *think* therefore I am' takes no account of feeling and will. We have won much in clarity of thought and understanding of the calculable elements in the world from this evolution to intellect. But it is proving a dead end. Man must himself, by self-development, undertake the next step in evolution, which will not be to a new mysticism, but to a conscious perception of the Spirit. Then he will be able to direct even his practical affairs and social institutions from living ideas.

To describe how this is being done in institutions of many kinds is the purpose of this book. It does not require that the workers in these institutions shall necessarily have developed higher powers of cognition in themselves. The unprejudiced healthy intellect is capable of grasping and working with 'living' ideas though it does not originate them. And an essential element in the 'living' ideas lies in the mobile picture of threefold man. We can immediately recognise how it must supplant the picture of man on which so many social institutions are based. In education, the child is commonly treated as an adult in miniature. The threefold picture of the child reveals his gradual attainment of adulthood in three rhythmically successive periods of about seven years. The first sees the unfolding of will activity. The child then lives in perpetual movement—even in his thinking he is concerned with what things do, or what you do with them. The second period finds him living in feeling, rhythm and imagination. His thinking is then really a heart thinking. Only in the third period—beginning with puberty—does he awake to modern intellectual consciousness, in which he is in danger of being imprisoned for life if the intellect has been awakened prematurely, and the forces of will and feeling have not been given proper guidance in his earlier life.

In the treatment of retarded children, again, the interplay of the three systems is an essential factor. If such a child is unable to concentrate, it is not through the head but through exercises with the limbs that the necessary will element may be brought into his thinking. Or to treat a child who has fixed ideas it is necessary to grasp the interrelation of the three systems in the process of memory. We become conscious of an idea or an impression in the head, but happily ideas do not remain in the head, or we would be distracted by a confusion of rampant memories. The conscious idea sinks into the unconscious metabolism, from where we evoke it in the act of memory. But if the metabolism is too weak to retain it, it will constantly rise into consciousness as a 'fixed' idea. The treatment is to strengthen the metabolism in such a way that it can retain the memory images until they are needed. Again, in medical treatment, it must be remembered that the plant is the threefold man in reverse. It is root substances that are related to the head, flower and fruit to the limbs, leaves to the central rhythmic system. Medicines given through digestion directly reach the metabolism, injections into the blood stream specially affect the rhythmic system, bath lotions work most effectively on the nervous system.

Such is an example of the approach to man in the institutions and activities described in this book. But there is one sphere in which Steiner's philosophy embraces the whole of human society, and gives an entirely new basis for a modern commonwealth. All previous societies have postulated the division of their members into groups or classes limited to the performance of different functions in the body social. Steiner saw that the demand for every man to be a complete man— which has grown so strongly in the past and present centuries—is now calling for the realisation of threefold man in a threefold state which is total man writ large. Every man is now concerned with the whole economic life, if not as a producer at least as a consumer; every man rightly demands to participate in the creations of the spirit in education, literature, the arts etcetera; every man demands a fair share of economic production, and equality before the law. These constitute three spheres of society, which Steiner called the Economic Sphere, the Spiritual Sphere and the Rights Sphere. What a modern, often cumbersome, democratic state requires is not evolution to one omnicompetent state, or devolution to small regional divisions, but the separation of the state into three spheres, each with its own characteristic organisation. The state then becomes the man writ large, not an organisation but an organism, in which harmony can become established through the very fact that each sphere finds its own organisation and character, just as heart, head and metabolism, while following their own laws, work together in the physical organism. It is not the job of the rights state, or parliament, to interfere with economic production or control education, or the job of economics to settle the claim on the products of industry (wages and salaries) or demand that schools and universities shall produce the kind of man they require.

In the State, as in the body of man, we must learn to distinguish where we cannot divide. The state will then function not as a Utopia, but as an organism in which confrontations can be met and disagreements adjusted in the right place and in the right way—in consultation between the three spheres. The proposal for such a threefold commonwealth was strenuously and publicly advocated by Steiner at the end of the First World War. It received much support, but the formal thinking—national omnicompetent states—of President Wilson won the day. There was no ability to grasp the idea of a functional division.

Today, however, as this volume shows, the movement to found institutions, based on such functional destinations as are the essence of threefold man, is ever on the increase. They will surely in time produce such a climate of thinking as may lead to the acceptance of the idea of a threefold state, without which there seems small hope of the continuance of a free society.

FURTHER READING

Rudolf Steiner, *Theosophy—An Introduction to the Supersensible Knowledge of the World and the Destination of Man* (Rudolf Steiner Press, London, 1973)

Rudolf Steiner/Owen Barfield, *The Case for Anthroposophy* (Rudolf Steiner Press, London, 1970)

Rudolf Steiner, *Occult Science—An Outline* (Rudolf Steiner Press, London, 1963)

Rudolf Steiner, *The Threefold Social Order* (Anthroposophic Press Inc., N.Y., 1972)

Rudolf Steiner, *The Social Future* (Anthroposophic Press Inc., N.Y., 1972)

Rudolf Steiner, *The Inner Aspect of the Social Question* (Rudolf Steiner Press, London, 1950)

3. THE ARTS IN LIFE

by ARNE KLINGBORG

How often today we hear of the need to give attention to the creative individual. Society and life in general bring us tasks which demand creative activity.

In connection with education and teaching on all levels, many people believe that the overall objectives must be concerned with awakening the creative individual. Research has shown that it is the encouragement of creative ability, and not the accumulation of knowledge or 'book learning', which calls forth productive endeavour. Our teaching, even the traditional academic teaching methods, have one-sidedly encouraged the student's receptive talents at the cost of the creative ones. Time and time again we are faced with tasks which show that creative ability is necessary for developing a functional, overall view of complicated situations. Such a view is needed for large social questions as well as for the often complicated tasks of everyday life.

These experiences show the necessity for a radical reconsideration of our entire method of educating, from elementary school to university level, so that all teaching becomes the furthering of creativity, the developing of creativity, instead of the opposite, which now so often prevails. Many people are convinced that such a reconsideration must be demanded absolutely if we are to ward off social developments which are now moving toward ultimate catastrophe.

But at the same time as from many sides we are made attentive to the creative individual, we are aware of powerful influences which refuse to recognise creative capacities in human beings and try with forceful arguments to persuade us that our actions are invariably the outcome of external stimuli. It can easily be seen how the way of thinking practised by these Behaviourists tends towards depriving the individual of his dignity as a creative being, with a potentiality for freedom, and reducing him to passivity and resignation. We are in the midst of a struggle where the creative possibilities inherent in the individual are exposed to destructive attacks. It is a war—Jacques Lusseyran speaks of it—against the individual self.

Faced with these attacks, we become uncertain; we have no adequate concepts for describing the creative self; we ask ourselves: what do we mean by the creative individual?

In the past the term 'creative ability' was linked to the artist's power to create. Today we speak of the creative individual in a much wider sense. It is not the occupational artist who comes immediately to mind, but the creative ability which exists, at least as a possibility, in every person.

It is interesting to follow Herbert Read's train of thought when, after the Second World War, he occupied himself intensively with the question of the creative individual. With the shattering experiences of the war behind him, he felt that we must be attentive to the new tasks that life was placing before us. We had to find a new relationship to the moral life, our responsible actions in life and in society.

Earlier there was the moral or the noble life, more or less linked with moral prescriptions, commandments and laws, and adherence to them could be brought about by means of the threat of punishment and eternal condemnation. Now commandments from the old style of life, the laws concerning how man should act have been replaced by rational planning on scientific lines. We are told that from rational points of view we must act in this way or that. A style of life which in the beginning sought to be in the common interest of all has developed more and more into a life-style for robots. The individual is forced into simple, stereotyped patterns of action and is steered without being able to find out how. We may expect a reaction in terms of unrestrained out-pouring of primitive aggression-urges if the individual pays no heed to his own creative possibilities.

The modern individual must become morally productive; the moral act must become a spontaneous act of the will.

In the dramatic situation of our time, viewed at a time of moral sickness, Herbert Read sees no possibility of deliverance through organisational, external measures. Spiritual means alone can bring healing. An aesthetic upbringing, he suggests, can lead to a new, up-to-date morality:

> Through art a possibility exists to channel and develop the individual's instinctive energy into productive paths, so that no inhibitions arise which can have a devastating effect on his development. Through art the individual learns how he can develop himself and for the first time become free; that is to say, morally productive.*

In the experience of his creative possibilities the individual regains his dignity as a person.

There are two important points which Herbert Read particularly develops. First, he widens the old conception of art to include creative, productive activity in general. The experience of creative activity is at the same time the experience of a free, spontaneous act of the will—an experience which must be carried further if the individual is to be able to change the world or to bring healing to a sick world. Herbert Read's second point is that through art the individual learns how he can develop himself.

The artist, the creative individual, stands before a material which he tries to shape and transform in a meaningful way. He has a feeling for the possibilities inherent in the material. But he also stands before himself; he has a feeling for possi-

* Herbert Read: *Education Through Art*. Faber & Faber, 1958

bilities, sees difficulties, and has to relate himself creatively to conditions of his own life.

Herbert Read's reflections lead towards intimate problems: the experience of the human self in the field of creative possibilities, where at the same time it is a question of the self transforming itself, of being creative in relationship to itself, if its actions are to be productive in large social contexts.

In *Education Through Art*, Herbert Read refers to the artistic, creative experience, but as an authority on modern art he is at the same time somewhat reserved when faced with the modern artistic expression. It is not easy to refer to art as a healing force when we find so much destruction expressed in modern art—to such a degree that acts of destruction are actually represented as a mode of artistic expression! Is a renewal of art necessary before one can speak of art as a healing force in life?

Herbert Read does not go into this question, but in order to make clear what he means by the creative capacity of the human individual he draws attention to an all but completely forgotten small work—Friedrich Schiller's *Twenty-seven Letters on the Aesthetic Education of Man*, published in 1795.

After the French Revolution, with all that he experienced of its possibilities and disappointments, Schiller formulates his contribution to the realisation of the great 'freedom ideal'. Involved in Kant's philosophy, but at odds with Kant's view of duty as the highest manifestation of human morality, and enlivened by the meeting with Goethe, Schiller searches for the region where the individual can be free and morally productive.

First, he shows how we are subject to the necessity of the sensuous life, its fluctuations and demands. Here we meet the whole range of passions, appetites and impulses; here is life with its continually shifting forms and its insatiability. In this sphere we are more or less slaves to our urges and instincts, however necessary they are for our existence. We tend to become children of nature.

Faced, however, with this great variety of continual change, we seek for that which is regulated by law and has a stable, enduring character. We study relationships, and with our logical intellect we formulate laws. We use some of these laws for gaining control over nature. On the same logical grounds we formulate laws for living together. The 'moral necessity' demands this or that of us. We order, we reckon, we develop our systems. Out of logical necessity we find reasons why we ought to act in this way or in that. Here again we are subject to a necessity which excludes freedom. We are subject to the rational impulse which is rooted in human nature. We are subject to the urge for form.

Where the urge for form prevails, life tends to stagnation, dogmatism, formalism, conservatism. If the urge for the sensuous gains the upper hand, life tends toward the dissolution of form. It is characterised by chance and caprice; the egotistical whim becomes decisive.

In our actions we swing between these two extremes. From one aspect we can say that through heredity, inherited disposition, biological conditions, we are in the stream to which the urge for the sensuous belongs. On the other side, our lives are shaped by the environment, by established behaviour-patterns and the work of earlier generations. Here, in Schiller's language, we meet the 'urge for form'. Hence we meet two realms; both are necessary for our existence, but our dependence on them involves us in all sorts of problems.

Have we then no possibility of freedom? Are we only the result of biological inheritance and cultural environment? Is freedom a great illusion, limited to a possible freedom of choice among fixed alternatives?

Schiller now turns to the realm where the individual, through his own activity, annuls the inexorable necessity of the urge for the sensuous and the urge for form. This is the realm where the individual creates, where he shapes, where he is 'artist' and 'player'. Here he is bound to neither urge. He avails himself of both and brings them into harmony.

As a creative person the individual starts with material from the realm of the senses, but he gives it a new form, a meaningful shape. Or he starts with a given necessity from the side of the urge for form, and through his creative activity he brings the form to life. In so doing, he creates. He is free.

For Schiller, freedom is not an abstraction; freedom is creative activity. The moral person is productive. Through his creative activity he can give life to that in the law which he understands to be correct; and he can try to change those aspects of law which do not take into account the creative individual. Through free creative activity he can overcome the egotism in the realm of the natural urges, and himself become more truly social, capable of interest for others and human sympathy, not because he is forced to it but because he wishes it himself.

Schiller was certain that the 'urge to play', creative ability, is a fundamental part of every person, and this gave him the power and enthusiasm to speak also of a State fit for human beings. Thus he spoke of three social forms: In the 'ethical state', the individual will is subjected to the general will through force of law and duty. At the opposite pole is the 'dynamic state', in which the sensual urges are tamed by violence. Between these two, Schiller sees hope for the 'aesthetic state', built on the artistic capacities of the human being to unite and harmonise both poles freely:

> The dynamical state can only make society possible, while restraining nature by nature; the ethical state can only make it (morally) necessary, while subjecting the single to the universal will; the aesthetic state alone can make it actual, since it fulfils the will of the whole through the nature of the individual. If need already impels man to

society, and reason plants social principles within him, yet Beauty alone can impart to him a *social character* . . .*

When today we read Schiller's *Letters* and note how he uses the words 'beauty', or 'the urge to play', we have to try very actively to come to grips with what lies behind the words which over the years have become worn out and misused.

Beauty is the far-reaching concept which in itself embraces creative activity and the element of freedom. Beauty is an expression of the free creative act. The urge to play exists in human nature as a disposition, and it is here that freedom should be first aroused. This is the goal of education. The free act, the activity of art, does not exist by natural necessity. If it did, the act could not be free. It must be awakened by each individual. A human community which attends to the creative possibilities in every person develops a sense for true human dignity. Knowledge regarding the human person has been one-sidedly cultivated around the concepts of heredity and environment. Schiller is exploring a new outlook.

Once the tension which Schiller shows to exist has been recognised, productive discoveries can be made concerning private life, the development of art, and different tendencies in contemporary cultural life. One can well understand Herbert Read's enthusiasm when faced with Schiller's findings.

The endeavours of many modern artists at the beginning of this century can be seen as a search for the source of creative activity. How many artists tried to free themselves from a burdensome tradition, with its stereotyped concepts regarding beauty and art, where education in painting consisted first in reproducing nature and in schooling the eye by copying classical art? How many artists led us into the field of tension of which Schiller spoke, but in which the

* *The Philosophical and Aesthetic Letters and Essays of Schiller*, translated J. Weiss (John Chapman, 1845), Letter 27

artists in their search came to swing between the two extremes? So Picasso and Braque took us through cubism, and Juan Gris, Mondrian, and Malevitsch, through their cool, clean, more and more abstract works, to the worlds where they sought that conformity to law which lies behind the forms of the created world. In their attempts they tended towards the pole of the urge for form. Through Miro, Max Ernst, Salvador Dali, we were thrown down into the depths of the seething unconscious processes of life where the artists hoped to find the sources of creative activity. A movement began which tended towards the pole of the urge for the sensuous and continued into the large field of spontaneous 'happenings' and psychedelic fantasies. As we come closer to the field where the creative possibilities exist, we find ourselves also in a force-field where we can easily fall into one-sidedness if we are unable to hold the balance between the poles of which Schiller speaks.

One of the artists at the Bauhaus, Lothar Schreier, described the situation in the following way: 'We know that through modern art, as a sign of a new turning-point in the world, there has opened the world of darkness as well as the world of light. Through us, demons and angels work in the human world.'

*　　*　　*

In the development of modern art the work of Rudolf Steiner forms a unique element. Rudolf Steiner made his mark at first as a philosopher, and as a scholar and commentator on the scientific works of Goethe. He then moved on to develop his 'spiritual science'—Anthroposophy—and through it made a crucial contribution to the question of the creative individual and the roll of art in life. Many artists at work during the first two decades of this century could link themselves to Steiner's ideas. This is made evident, among other things, in notes left by Kandinsky in which one can see the great influence Steiner had on this Russian artist's conception of art. Steiner later made his appearance as an artist of exceptional versatility in his own right. He worked as dramatist, creator of a new art of movement—Eurythmy, as architect, sculptor, painter, and poet. But he remained largely unknown as an artist, at least in public circles. It seems that his work was looked upon more as a curiosity developed by an eccentric personality, with significance only for a special private circle. It is only in later years that his artistic work has been given more and more attention.

If one follows Steiner's artistic work, one can make many interesting observations. One of the most striking is that he always created in a social context, never with abstract, exhibitive purposes in mind. His work always came out of a concrete situation in life. The Mystery Dramas were written when there was a circle of people who needed them and wished to produce them in München right away. The language of form in his architecture was developed at Dornach when a group of people, artists and amateurs, came together to provide him with practical assistance in this field.

Thus we see Rudolf Steiner in the unique situation of being simultaneously researcher, artist, and teacher. While occupied with the building of the first Goetheanum he continued to work out the research results of Spiritual Science in a conceptual form by means of lectures, and at the same time he gave advice and illustrative help to the growing circle of fellow-workers.

The research in Anthroposophy forms the background for his artistic activity. Anthroposophy shows that in every person there are possibilities for developing organs which can give direct experience of spiritual realities. The human self can experience itself as spirit when it realises that it can relate creative development to its own being. 'Anthroposophy becomes an artistic road which can lead the spiritual

Wooden sculpture 'The Representative of Humanity' by Rudolf Steiner.

Detail from the large clay model for 'The Representative of Humanity'.
The upward-striving Lucifer.

Detail from the large clay model for 'The Representative of Humanity'.
The upper Ahriman.

Rudolf Steiner, Dornach, 1913.

in man to the spiritual in the universe.' This finding implies
that in every person there dwells an artist in the widest
sense. One's being as an artist is not only an ability received
through inheritance; it can also be awakened and developed.
Art becomes a broadly human, universal concern, not
something which affects only a chosen circle of gifted
people. From this standpoint one can begin again to have the
feeling that a new folk-art is in the making.

In connection with the artistic activity at the Goetheanum
construction site, Rudolf Steiner directs the attention of his
fellow-workers time and time again, both in conversations
and in lectures, to the new way of relating oneself to the
material which stands at the artist's disposal.

We are indeed already living in an age when this penetration into the
spiritual flow of the powers of nature—that is to say of the spiritual
powers behind nature—must begin. It must again be possible for us
not merely to look at colours, to reproduce them outwardly here or
there, but to live with colour, to experience the inner life-force of
colour. This cannot be done by merely studying in painting, for
instance, the effects of the colours and their interplay as we look at
them. It can only be done if once again we sink our soul in the flow of
red or blue, for instance, if the flow of the colour really lives—if we are
able to ensoul the essence of colour that instead of evolving any kind
of colour symbolism (which would of course be the very opposite way
of going to work) we really discover what is living in colour just as the
power of laughter exists in a man who laughs. Hence we must seek out
the paths of return to the flowing world of colour . . . If (man) has no
other perception save 'here is red, here is blue'—which is often the
case today—he can never press onwards to living experience of the
real essence of colour . . . We must know how to surrender the whole
soul to what speaks to us from out of colour. Then, when we are confronted with red we have a sense of attack, aggression . . . Blue has an
element that seems to pass away from us, to leave us, something after
which we gaze with a certain wistfulness, with yearning . . .

It must be the endeavour of art again to dive down into the life of
the elements. Art has observed and studied nature long enough, has
tried long enough to solve all the riddles of nature and to express in
another form all that can be observed by this penetration into nature.
What lives in the elements is, however, dead so far as modern art is
concerned. Air, water, light—all are dead as they are painted today;
form is dead as is expressed in modern sculpture. A new art will arise

49

when the human soul learns to penetrate to the depths of the elemental world, for this world is *living* . . .*

Rudolf Steiner recommends a completely new method of training: the artist must enter into the material with self-knowledge. When he does so he will activate definite experiences of the self. The first self, designed to think and speculate, will observe how easy it is to move towards abstractions. Time and time again he will reveal himself by looking upon the experiences of colour in a symbolic way, and, instead of entering into the creative possibilities in the world of colour, he will fashion his experiences into abstract colour-schemes. Another self, involved more in the realm of feelings, will perhaps nearly lose itself in rapture when faced with the possibilities of colour, or will again and again reveal itself by attempting to express life by means of the colours, instead of entering into a perceptive, listening relationship with them. In the course of such training the artist will be repeatedly shaken by coming face to face with his own one-sidedness. He sees that he himself may be an obstacle to the artistic experience; that he must overcome this one-sidedness in order to connect his entire self with his material so that 'through what we make and do there will speak not only we ourselves, but also the creative forces that are active in the world'.

The task of creating an equilibrium between two poles of man's being was embodied by Steiner in his great piece of sculpture, on which he worked with a collaborator, Edith Maryon, over a period of years. This shows a central figure, the 'Representative of Humanity', standing between two powerful beings, of whom he spoke often in lectures, Lucifer and Ahriman. The figure of Lucifer embodies the desire-nature of man as it surges up and dissolves order into fantasy

* Rudolf Steiner, *Ways to a New Style in Architecture*, Lecture 5, given at Dornach July 26th, 1914 (Anthroposophical Publishing Company, London, 1927)

and tempts to escapism. The figure of Ahriman embodies the dry, cold world of an intellect which would reduce all human life to death. In physiological terms, this same polarity comes to expression in the fever of the blood contrasted with the sclerotic tendencies of nerve and bone. Our daily lives entail a constant search for balance between these extremes, between the excessively fantastic, and the coldness of abstract logic.

After a series of preliminary studies for this sculpture, a full-scale plasticine model was realised. It became the point of departure for the final design, in elm. However, with Rudolf Steiner's death in 1925 the monumental work was still unfinished. Standing before the nine-metre-high woodcarving, one can see that the central figure asserts itself in a most notable way. It detaches itself from the rest of the block and is stamped with a calm, advancing movement. The figure lifts its left hand with force; the right hand points downward. The forms are whole and flowing; they seem filled with power and tranquillity in relation to the surrounding figures, which are shaped in mobile, disorganised concavities on the one hand, and hardened, cramped forms on the other.

In a lantern-slide lecture* Rudolf Steiner described his method of creating the 'language of form' which comes out in the different figures. Before the model of the head of Ahriman, Steiner said, among other things, the following:

> An attempt has been made to shape the human countenance as if only the hardening, sclerosis-inducing forces of the ageing process were at work. In terms of the human soul the forces are those which make man a philistine, a pedant, a materialist; those forces through which he is an intellectual being.
>
> If within his soul man had no heart, but only intellect, he would display the physiognomy seen in the figure of Ahriman. One does not come to know man's being if one speaks of it only in terms of physiology

* Rudolf Steiner, *Der Baugedanke des Goetheanum* (Bern, June 29th, 1921)

and anatomy—they give only a one-sided knowledge of man. One must go further and grasp the form in an artistic way. Only then does one learn to know what lives and works in man, what he truly is.

... One must rise to a purely artistic outlook which is part of artistic cognizance—one must feel with Goethe when he says: 'He for whom Nature begins to display her evident secrets feels the deepest longing for her worthiest interpreter, Art.'

With regard to the Lucifer form Rudolf Steiner continued:

Man must enter completely into creative Nature if he wishes to work out sculpturally a work of art such as the Lucifer form. It is not a matter of working symbolically or allegorically, nor of thinking out a concept which then becomes clothed in the old language of form. Instead, one must become truly absorbed in Nature's creative process. One must come to know the nature of the human chest and lungs; the hearing organs, and the stunted wing organs in the shoulder-blades. All this must be placed into a completely different context. Man must be seen as if he were not primarily an intellectual being, but a being in which the heart has presumed to take the upper hand. Then the heart, the hearing organs, the wing-like organs, would build a whole.

Anyone who allows not only the naturalistic to apply, but also what exists ideally and spiritually as a possibility in the human being, comes to the art that sees, in Goethe's spirit, what can be revealed regarding the secrets of the world and of life.

The artist becomes absorbed in Nature's ideal possibilities, which allow themselves to be transformed, and so he can develop a language of form which in turn helps to reveal the ideals, the qualities, related to the essential nature of the world around him.

*　　*　　*

For Rudolf Steiner, art has a most important task in human existence. Through artistic forms, it is possible to depict the forces which work and create in the world as supersensible principles. In the sense-world man is, to begin with, separated from the origin of his being. The world is dead, or 'sick', as Herbert Read expresses it. Man must awaken once more his creative being, which brings him into harmony with the creative forces in the world. In this way he may long to be able to reveal through art, in sense-perceptible forms, his complete creative being and the forces which live and create in the world. Once he succeeds to some extent in doing this, he will learn from experience that artistic endeavour carries with it a healing power.

Research in spiritual science makes it possible to penetrate into a number of areas which in ordinary life are approached only on the first level of understanding. This is true even in the large field of activity where the processes of life go on. Through our own particular feeling for life we note if we are healthy or sick. This is illustrated in familiar phrases. We say, 'I am in good shape' when we are healthy and feeling well, or 'I am in bad shape', when we are sick. That is, we experience something of the force which holds the body upright, and keeps it in good condition when we are feeling well. These feelings are even more evident when our bodily forces do not bear us up and we feel poorly. In common experience it is clear that the forces of life are closely related to health and sickness, to growth and decay. During youth the human bodily form is filled with tension and vitality. With age the form slackens, or hardens into brittleness.

Rudolf Steiner describes what we all experience to some extent through this feeling for life as an expression of man's 'life-organism', a supersensible principle, a 'time body' or 'etheric body' which flows through our form and gives it shape. When raised into a clear and conscious form of spiritual perception, this organism is seen as a flowing, rhythmical force field of changing colours and forms.

It was this inner experience which captured the interest of Kandinsky when, at the beginning of this century, he studied the results of Rudolf Steiner's research. This gave him the impulse to develop out of inner supersensible experiences an up-to-date language of form primarily for painting. This development is apparent in his commentary on Steiner's writings, material which Sixten Ringbom has carried further in his book, *The Sounding Cosmos*.*

In 1911 Rudolf Steiner came face to face with a concrete question put by a person who had been absorbed in Steiner's research for many years, particularly regarding man's life-organism. Out of a definite life-situation this person asked: Is it not possible, through definite movements of and around the life-organism, which is the bearer of the rhythmical balance of health and sickness, to activate healing, strengthening, and regulating forces right down to the physical body? This question aroused Rudolf Steiner's enthusiasm and led on presently to a new art of movement, Eurythmy, chiefly by way of his investigations into human speech.

Our current language has tended increasingly to take on the character of dead information. But if we enter into language with the help, for example, of the great poets, we begin to have a feeling for their way of using those elements in language which we know as consonants and vowels; we see how the poets can create from the possibilities which exist in language itself. Steiner shows how, through the plosive, fricative, and sibilant sounds of the consonants, we are more linked with the forces and events of the world around us, while through the resounding, musical vowels we give expression to something which lives within the individual soul.

Our capacity to form language and to give it force depends upon the united action of our speech-organs and our life-organism. We can be aware of this co-operation when we are ill and feel how the strength of our speech diminishes. We can observe the same co-operation in children while they take to their mother-tongue and imitate sounds and words, and the rhythmic element in language is clearly apparent. Rudolf Steiner describes how in our entire

* Sixten Ringbom, *The Sounding Cosmos* (Åbo, 1970). (Not in English)

life-organism, through its close connection with speech-organs, rhythmical 'dancing' movements occur when we speak. This is true especially when we experience in speech the interplay between the vowels and the consonants.

It is possible to make visible the harmonious movements which our life-organism produces, or, in other words, to 'dance' the inner life of speech itself. The Eurythmy movements reveal the rhythmical gestures which are concealed in living language. With language as a starting-point, it was possible for Rudolf Steiner, together with Marie von Sievers (later Marie Steiner), and a number of young, enthusiastic fellow-workers to develop step by step the new art of movement.

Thus it happens that at the same time as new impulses for the plastic arts are arising with the construction of the first Goetheanum in Dornach, Rudolf Steiner is disclosing new ways toward a renewal of the art of speech, and, as a direct consequence, the new art-form, Eurythmy, emerges.

This happens during the time surrounding the First World War among a group of people from different nations, all of whom had experienced a pressing and urgent need for a new spiritual orientation. So a remarkable situation, unique in modern art-history, comes about. At one and the same place architects, sculptors and painters work together with helpers on the building's construction while at the same time, together with others, they exercise and train themselves in the art of speech and assist in the development of the new art of movement for the stage, all of which is done in temporary rooms and sheds on the construction site. Rudolf Steiner's artistic impulse is developed in a social community, and so an inspiring interaction arises between the building arts and the musical and dramatic arts. Out of the actual experience of a spiritual reality, working as a creative power in individual existence and in the world as a whole, the arts can once again be experienced in their reciprocal concurrence.

For anyone who has made himself familiar with, or has perhaps felt himself to be a participant in, the struggle of modern artists, it is more than impressive to see how Rudolf Steiner gives inspiration to a group of people and how his own efforts are awakened through active questions from this group. Such an impression is strengthened even more when one realises that this international group is composed of craftsmen, technologists, artists, and includes also many persons with no training in skilled labour or in the arts. Rudolf Steiner turns first not to established artists but to all who begin to experience art as an essential factor in life.

If it is possible, even as a very humble beginning, to create and shape from a new comprehensive view, or, better expressed, in accord with 'that which creates and works in the cosmos', then art will also work as a healing force in human existence, as Herbert Read and many with him feel and hope.

At the opening in Dornach of one of the studio buildings, which was to be used for etching the large, coloured-glass windows to be set into the Goetheanum structure, Rudolf Steiner spoke to his fellow-workers concerning the role of art.

In the present age man is more and more compelled to bring about order, stability, peace and harmony by means of external laws, decrees or institutions, definitions in words. This implies no syllable or thought of criticism, for it must be so in our age. But something must be added to this—something that signifies the onward evolution of humanity in a different sense. It is probable that our building will not be able fully to attain its goal—indeed we are only aiming at a primitive beginning. Yet if human culture is able to take what is expressed in our building . . . and develop it; if the ideas underlying such works of art find followers—then people who allow themselves to be impressed by these works of art and who have learnt to understand their language, will never do wrong to their fellow men either in heart or intellect, because the forms of art will teach them how to love; they will learn to live in harmony and peace with their fellow beings. Peace and harmony will pour into all hearts through these forms; such buildings will be 'Lawgivers' and their forms will be able to achieve what external institutions can never achieve.

... true redemption, the turning of evil into good, will in future depend upon whether true art is able to pour a spiritual fluid into the hearts and souls of men. When men's hearts and souls are surrounded by the achievements of true architecture, sculpture and the like, they will cease to lie if it happens they are untruthfully inclined; they will cease to disturb the peace of their fellow men if this is their tendency. Edifices and buildings will begin to *speak*, and in a language of which people today have no sort of inkling.*

*   *   *

The consequences of art as an active factor in life become fully evident through Rudolf Steiner's initiatives in education. When after the First World War, he worked out the guiding principles for an up-to-date pedagogy, it was the artistic element which permeated its teaching methods. For Steiner it is a matter not only of bringing as much artistic activity as possible into the school, as urged by Herbert Read; the essential factor is that the teaching as a whole becomes an art. The artistic element, in the comprehensive meaning already described, must then be taken seriously.

A spiritually scientific view of man brings out the essential phases in the process of growing up which we all go through on the way towards adulthood,† when we hope to establish independent thinking and creative social capacities. The little child, who is finding a relationship to his own body and to the world primarily by means of imitation, is to a high degree exposed to those impressions which he receives from his surroundings. Whatever we do will influence the child in the earliest years. The impressions the child receives and unconsciously imitates have consequences even in the building up of his bodily organs. Adults have a great task and a great responsibility. They have to create for the child a

* Rudolf Steiner, *Ways to a New Style in Architecture*, Lecture 2, given at Dornach, June 17th, 1914 (Anthroposophical Publishing Co., London, 1927)

† See also the fifth article in this volume: *Education—The Normal Child*, by Eileen Hutchins

worthy environment—meaningful, human and balanced. The entire environment created by parents and others who look after children can be healingly constructive, or it can be destructive.

The adult is himself part of the child's environment, his attitudes towards life also need to be formed into a living work of art, worthy of imitation.

When children begin school, anyone can see how they long to experience the world. Healthy children become strongly involved with everything they meet, reacting to it with sympathy or antipathy. The teaching should not be concerned merely with imparting a maximum of intellectual knowledge; the child must be enabled to experience the subject-matter of a lesson in such a way that it nourishes his soul. The teacher must work over his material like an artist, so that it becomes something that the children can experience. The artistic element must permeate the factual material itself. In the children who wish to experience the world the teacher meets the natural artist in all of us, in the broadest meaning of the word. The teacher must be able to speak to this artist. When he does so, the children will respond with creative activity. The child is not intended merely to carry in his head a supply of facts; he should come out of the educational experience with a capacity for action. Certainly it is important that the children should be active in artistic work, where they still unconsciously experience a capability which can be brought out. But the essential factor is that the teaching as a whole should take the artistic element so seriously that the complete person is addressed and his development helped.

At later ages the children wish not only to experience the world but also to understand it. They want to learn about the laws and relations in nature and the conditions for human co-existence. At these ages, teaching is permeated by a more scientific element. But a scientific element, when faced with the facts of life and evolution, can make use of art, which promotes the capacity to take in large contexts through pictures and sharpens attention to the active tendencies toward form in nature and in consciousness.

In these later ages art itself becomes the object of study. Through the history of the arts, and through an aesthetic which embraces artistic activity, art becomes comprehensible as an active factor in life.

A school which sees as its task the bringing up of children and young people to become free, independent, discerning, creative persons, full of initiative, must take art seriously. In turn, art must constantly renew itself from a comprehensive picture of humanity. It must free itself from isolation in galleries and art-shops and open up possibilities for a new 'folk art'. This is the art which can provide a creative activity in which every person can more and more feel himself a participant, and out of which he can come to recognise his own experiences in life.

At the time of the founding of the first Waldorf School in Stuttgart, Rudolf Steiner said:

> If our society were to be permeated, even through the upbringing of children, with a social art, a true culture of the will would be brought about. No one can 'will'—act freely—who has not cultivated the will through a genuinely artistic upbringing. To recognise this secret concerning the relationship between art and life, especially in connection with the springs of human action, will be one of the very first demands of a future, psychological pedagogy; and all future pedagogy must be psychological.*

Thus in Steiner's work we find a way to a renewal of art which can permeate the whole of human and social life. Steiner began to realise in practice, and from a much richer perspective, what Schiller had glimpsed as a possibility and a hope. He gave an impulse which, after a further half century of work since his death, is very much alive. Social and

---

* Rudolf Steiner, *Geisteswissenschaftliche Behandlung sozialer und pädogogischer Fragen* (Stuttgart, April 21st–September 28th, 1919)

artistic developments during this period have amply confirmed that he was pointing to a way which leads into the heart of the true spiritual and social needs of this century.

FURTHER READING

Herbert Read, *Education Through Art* (Faber & Faber, London, 1958)

Rudolf Steiner, *Ways to a New Style in Architecture* (Anthroposophical Publishing Co., London, 1927)

Rudolf Steiner, *Colour* (Rudolf Steiner Press, London, 1971)

Rudolf Steiner, *The Arts and their Mission* (Anthroposophic Press Inc., N.Y., 1964)

Rudolf Steiner, *Art in the Light of Mystery Wisdom* (Rudolf Steiner Press, London, 1970)

Rudolf Steiner, *A Lecture on Eurythmy* (Rudolf Steiner Press, London, 1967)

M. Raffé, A. C. Harwood and M. Lundgren, *Eurythmy and the Impulse of Dance* (Rudolf Steiner Press, London, 1974)

Rudolf Steiner, *Speech and Drama* (Anthroposophical Publishing Co., London, 1959)

Maria Schindler, *Goethe's Theory of Colour Applied* (New Knowledge Books, East Grinstead, 1964)

Arild Rosenkrantz, *A New Impulse in Art* (New Knowledge Books, East Grinstead, 1967)

4. ARCHITECTURE

Buildings for Life

by REX RAAB

Work arising! That is just how a builder or an architect feels when he sees the walls of a building rising from the newly laid foundations. He senses that his own and others' labour in planning or executing a design is a contribution to the community at large and is destined to be of use for generations to come.

In his approach to building, Rudolf Steiner did not, like so many of his younger contemporaries, merely develop ideas on architecture which were doomed to remain largely unbuilt, or were even unbuildable. For him the need and the intention to build came first; then the ideas corresponding with the nature of the task; then the solution and execution itself; and only then a further elaboration of principles thoroughly supported by practice. Steiner's influence on the architecture of our times has been both direct—through his buildings—and indirect—through his idea on the way to achieve a new architecture. This influence is more or less easily traceable.

Imagine a group of teachers needing school premises, doctors wanting to found a clinic, or remedial educationists setting up a curative home for handicapped children or adults. Their aim must be a design which embodies a correspondence between the buildings and the activities

61

they will house. The architectural environment has a powerful influence on the well-being of the human beings in it. If the built spaces are right, they can powerfully support the work in hand; if they are wrong, they will hinder it at every turn—perhaps in subtle and insidious ways that remain unnoticed for a long time. This is where the architect comes in, and where he must prepare himself to meet the challenge of architectural and social reality simultaneously.

Eero Saarinen, the Finnish-American architect, saw architecture as the totality of our man-made physical surroundings, and showed that it is a matter of historical accident if the architect practises only on a narrow segment of his wide keyboard. By the same token, the scope and nature of building work directly serving anthroposophical activity has so far been mainly in the service of schools, medical centres (clinics, hospitals, sanatoria etcetera) churches and homes for the Christian Community, and a certain amount of private domestic architecture for individual clients. There has been little opportunity so far to work in commercial and industrial fields. Nor have city and regional planning yet proved open to anthroposophical impulses. The basic approach, though, is applicable to any architectural task. New activities create new social situations, and thus bring new tasks for the architect. He has to create a suitable sheath for new social forms. He should never aim for novelty for its own sake.

*   *   *

The origins of the new impulse Steiner gave to architecture lie in the two major buildings on which he worked during his life time. The second of these, in reinforced concrete, was begun shortly before his death. He could hear the sounds issuing from the site even when he could no longer supervise the works from the studio where he lay during his last months. This building was completed three and a half years after his death, and still stands on a hill above Dornach, near Basle in Switzerland, where it serves as the headquarters of the General Anthroposophical Society. Its predecessor, the first 'Goetheanum', on the same site, burned down during the New Year's night of 1922–3.

What manner of buildings were these? Why were they necessary? How did they come to be built? In what way do they represent a new impulse in architecture?

Steiner started with the basic spiritual nature of man, and with the need to strengthen and develop it. The Goetheanum was to be an example of a 'spiritual workshop' (his expression), where knowledge, art and social life could be woven together in a heightened form. It was to be a place for a true renewal and celebration of human festivals, born out of profound spiritual insight and creative effort. A building of this sort, the prototype of the kind of centre every community of the future will require if it is to remain mentally sound and socially effective, had quite naturally to incorporate a complete integration of the arts. To bring about such a synthesis, the origin and task of each individual art had to be investigated. Then they could be reconciled and act in harmony. To have achieved this to a high degree in the first Goetheanum, despite the fact that Steiner himself invariably spoke of it as a 'primitive beginning', is what gives him a title to fame as an architect.

The first Goetheanum was constructed of timber on a concrete base, with two rotundas of unequal diameter, and twin interlocking domes, reaching 110 feet high. The domes were clad in Norwegian slate, which shone silvery in the Jura landscape. Its successor, in reinforced concrete, interpretes the entire natural surroundings with singular power. It is a larger, though simpler, building, created as a home for a school of spiritual science, and surrounded by ancillary structures fulfilling various functions. These buildings have frequently been discussed in the architectural journals.

Further development was much retarded by the political and economic events of the late 1920s and '30s, and by the Second World War. But from the 1950s onwards, there has been a rapid expansion of work in the fields already mentioned. The first new building layout for a complete Waldorf school was realised in 1950 by Felix Kayser in Rendsburg. Since then, there has been much activity in several parts of the world. Some of the chief examples of consistent building schemes for Steiner schools are listed at the end of this essay.

All the schemes for such schools have to provide for an unusually wide variety of activities. Besides the normal classrooms (and there may be two or even three parallel classes for each year), together with their supporting specialist and other ancillary areas, there will be a need for eurythmy studios (a compulsory subject in the Steiner curriculum), and, as a rule, for additional facilities for music, art, remedial eurythmy and speech training. In many schools on the European continent, especially where State support has been forthcoming, the workshop sectors have often been developed beyond the usual craft lessons, to provide fully fledged training in carpentry, metal work, mechanics etcetera. Moreover, the rudiments of many other trades and skills form part of the regular curriculum. Such work prevents premature specialisation, and may also help in choosing a next step after school. The most ambitious undertaking in this direction to date is the Hibernia-Schule (see p. 76).

There can be no such thing as a properly functioning Steiner school without a hall and stage—or, in the pioneer stage, their improvised equivalents. This, the largest 'class room' on the school premises, is the heart and kernel of the school's life, its chief 'spiritual workshop', where the fruits of classroom work can be shared, and the whole life of the school community enriched and fostered.

Much current work is focused on curative education in all

64

The first Goetheanum 1913–23, Dornach, Switzerland. Interior view looking
east. Architect: Rudolf Steiner.

The first Goetheanum 1913–23, Dornach, Switzerland, from the south, and staircase inside. Architect: Rudolf Steiner.

The existing Goetheanum, opened 1928, from the south-west. Architect: Rudolf Steiner.

The 'Eurythmeum', Dornach, from the north-east. Architect: Rudolf Steiner.

West view of Engelberg Waldorf School. Architects: Raab and Klein.

The "New Church" in Berlin Wilmersdorf. Interior view. Architects: Laver and Raab. Mural 9 × 13·5 metres: Arne Klingborg.

its branches. Schools for mentally handicapped and maladjusted children are most often residential. Their central aims are not intellectual attainment, but the fostering of practical work and a full community life, steeped in a strong devotional mood. In such an environment, healing and social progress can go forward. These needs call for much sympathetic understanding from the architect called upon to design and equip appropriate spaces. Bayes working from England; Asmussen and Klingborg working from Sweden; Tschakalow working from Switzerland; Lauer, Seyfert, Raab working from Germany have, amongst others, been responsible for planning some larger remedial centres of consistent architectural interest, in various European countries.

The work of the Camphill Architects Group, centred in Botton, Yorkshire, deserves particular attention, because it has undertaken work in three continents, in each of which very different conditions are met. Gabor Tallo and Joan de Ris Allen have been responsible, severally and together, for work in South Africa, the United States and Great Britain, including Robert's House in Hermanus at the Cape; Beaver Run in Pennsylvania; Copake in New York State; and the centres in Scotland, Gloucestershire, Hampshire and Yorkshire.

The pattern is similar in many cases, but the solution varies according to climate and other factors. Providing for handicapped adults, rather than children, again brings new tasks. The trend here is towards the creation of 'villages', complete with production workshops and other facilities which allow each individual to make a contribution to the functioning of the whole. Here the Village Hall becomes a multi-purpose Community Centre. Besides this social gathering point, such village communities give rise to needs for a nursery school and school premises, dwelling houses, hostels for up to twenty-five persons, workshops, chapels, facilities for physical training and, frequently, farming and market gardening.

Doctors practising on lines initiated by Rudolf Steiner have developed their work furthest, so far, in Germany, Switzerland and Holland. This has brought opportunities to build clinics, hospitals, nursing homes, medical research centres and facilities for the manufacture of medicines and pharmaceutical products. The pioneering venture was the Ita Wegman Klinik in Arlesheim near Basle (formerly the Klinisch-Therapeutisches Institut, of which Steiner was co-founder), and its offshoot for cancer therapy, the Lukas Klinik nearby.

A general hospital on a communal basis has been operating for some years at Herdecke on the eastern edge of the Ruhr District. The manner in which it came into being, through the powerful collaboration of a group of medical doctors and an experienced architect, is itself an expression of the dynamics of this undertaking, which has set itself the task, among other things, of clinically and conclusively demonstrating the efficacy of the medicaments developed in anthroposophical medicine and of the whole approach to therapy that goes with them. The buildings are simple but adequate, with a character of their own, and turned out to be, by current standards of hospital building, sensationally cheap! Considerable extensions are now in progress. At the time of writing, plans are well advanced for a second major medical establishment in Germany, the Filder Klinik near Stuttgart.

The Weleda Company, which produces medicines and pharmaceuticals for anthroposophical doctors, is one of the very few commercial undertakings in the world which has been able to draw from the same source the inspiration for its products, for its research and production methods, and for the design of its factories and administrative offices. From such beginnings, something more considerable could grow, and will hopefully make a contribution towards mending the schizophrenic character of modern civilisation.

Adult education and teacher training are bringing new tasks. It is beginning to be obvious that a good deal of unrest and general demoralisation among students are linked with the kind of physical and architectural environment in which they live and work. Still on a small scale, but developing rapidly, are several centres of adult education based on Steiner's work, and which have already acquired their own architectural note. Apart from the Goetheanum itself, there are the Rudolf Steiner Seminariet at Järna near Stockholm, Emerson College in Sussex, and the teachers' training centre and the young people's Seminar in Stuttgart, the home of the first Waldorf School. It is too soon to write of the architectural consequences of more recent foundations of this type, but Eurythmy training and other branches of art training promise to bring the architect interesting new problems.

Old people's homes, and nursery and preschool centres bring problems spanning education, medicine and social life. An appreciable contribution has been made here. The need for more Kindergartens founded on a spiritual concept of man is a desperate one and the Steiner school movement is doing what it can to cope. The provision of a suitable environment at such a decisive stage in child development belongs to the programme of architectural work in hand. The experience gained in working specifically for schools and homes run on Steiner lines proves entirely relevant in a wider context. The author of this essay was recently approached by a Roman Catholic church congregation wishing to set up a nursery school in their parish. It was recognised that the impulse of anthroposophical architects is not to embody an ideology in their work, but to meet the true needs of children and bring a truly human quality into the environment. The author insisted on, and was granted, the

67

freedom to work with similar harmonies of straight and curved architectural forms, and with colour schemes etcetera corresponding to the needs of the very young, that he had introduced in work for Rudolf Steiner schools. An entirely satisfactory collaboration proved possible.

The real needs of old people are seldom met by moving them into new quarters termed a 'Retirement Home', or something similar. The elderly still have a very real contribution to make to the community, and a very real opportunity to go on growing as human beings. Rather than 'retiring' from the world, they are really entering their third (and with any luck, wisest!) phase of life, and they should be consulted in this capacity. Rather than being encouraged to withdraw altogether they should be given an opportunity, according to their needs and capabilities, to take an active interest and part in life from their new vantage point, where outer activity may be reduced, but inner activity can be correspondingly enhanced. Such an approach, which is not theory, but the result of observation, profoundly modifies any planning task set in this field. Moreover, it promotes a golden opportunity for making exciting new discoveries about one's fellow men through intensified collaboration at the exploratory stage. True activity—spiritual activity—comes into its own, lending a new touch of life to the treatment of every detail, large and small, which must be considered before the new quarters are built and can begin to function.

A current project embracing most of the tasks dealt with is the Educational-Social Centre in Dortmund. Here a conscious effort is being made to meet certain growing social needs and to bridge the gulf between the younger and older generations. The centre involves a complex grouping of functions, spaces and masses to serve both educational and social needs. It includes the rapidly-growing Dortmund Rudolf Steiner School for 1,100 children; an old people's home for about 230 persons; a social centre providing, besides the normal facilities, art therapy, physiotherapy and a catering department to provide the entire centre and the public with good quality food; a nursery school and pre-school centre with four groups of twenty-five to thirty children; a training school for social workers and teachers in this field; and living accommodation for some of the supporting staff and their families. A communal practice for six medical doctors is also envisaged. The school has already started on the new site.

*　　*　　*

A central architectural question contained in all these projects is that of the relation between form and function. The views of architects vary greatly in this matter—to the point of confusion and frustration. Steiner has made a major contribution to unravelling this problem both in theory and in practice.

To stress the importance of form does not mean to indulge in mere formalism. Everything in the world comes to meet us clothed in a particular form. Formlessness, which can only be relative, can never be a healthy goal, any more than the blind acceptance of too rigid a form. To leave something unformed will inevitably mean that we have fought shy of the task we have been set. The form we give a thing, however, will only be a true solution for the given problem if it is the product of a living process and continues to live and make a living experience possible after this process has been brought to a conclusion. Hence the constant aim among architects and designers who orientate themselves through anthroposophy is to find an 'organic' solution and a 'living' form.

Steiner pointed to two quite specific techniques in achieving this goal and was himself their exponent. In learning to grasp the function of a given architectural task he encouraged the architect to ask himself 'what happens?' In this way human experience is involved in the inquiry from the start and a solution can be found which does not exclude the human being which the building is to serve.

Even more specifically, 'metamorphosis', the transformation of mass and shape according with a recognisable motive or theme appropriate to the task, creates 'the appearance of consciousness'. And who would deny that it is an enhancement of consciousness which is required by modern conditions at every turn? With regard to the treatment of surface in architecture and sculpture Steiner pointed to the significance of the double curvature of the surface, to the 'twice bent plane', and showed that this creates 'the appearance of life'. (He never tired of illustrating what he meant by manipulations of his hat or gloves, if no other means were at his disposal.)

The relationship of form and material, and material and construction, are issues of a similar kind, urgently requiring to be resolved and constantly being impressed upon the anthroposophically active architect. He becomes aware of the fact that certain habits of thought that have grown up within the past hundred years or so must now be metamorphosed if progress is to be made and freedom reached.

A part of the tasks ahead will lie in facing the problems that have been uncovered. But they are not exhausted by this. Those versed in economic affairs are constantly seeking ways of financing 'the free spiritual life' and consequently of making construction programmes possible. Resourceful people in Sweden, Holland and Germany have already been able to create certain organs of expression in this direction. But there will probably never be a more faithful method than voluntary support. The first Goetheanum was erected entirely on this basis, entailing great personal generosity and sacrifice. That its successor was partially financed by fire insurance money was a factor which, for Steiner, had to be taken into consideration in the very character of the new design. As it turned out, the second building too would not have been completed without the enthusiasm of the treasurer and the intensified support of the members of the Anthroposophical Society.

The answer to the falling off of skill in the building trades and the mechanisation of construction techniques, together with the difficulties of financing already discussed, is more and more becoming: 'Do it yourself.' The Goetheanum was itself erected by the society as contractor. Emerson College has set up both its own planning office and a construction company which is already in operation and gaining valuable experience. This is a symptom that promises a great future.

A third immediate task consists in trying to meet the growing interest and needs of students who are beginning to look to anthroposophy for help in their work. Academic art training has plainly lost all vitality, attraction and relevance to recognisable contemporary tasks. Experience is beginning to show that training in architecture and art generally cannot be divorced from practice, and that anthroposophical methods and tasks lend themselves to this situation, stimulating invention and promoting a strong social element. Conferences that set themselves practical artistic tasks are opening up the way to more continuous, consolidated and consistent working situations.

A fourth task ahead lies in learning better to understand the effects of buildings on Nature and on human nature, and to take them into account in planning and building. The contemporary world has more or less stumbled on this complex problem. To make progress, the split between 'planning' and 'landscaping' must be gradually eliminated, just as the century-old rift between 'architecture' and 'engineering' must also be overcome.

Embracing all these tasks is the most essential of all, the integration of all the arts. This entails an attitude of mind, not an elaborate programme that can be dispensed

71

with if the economic situation appears unfavourable. Partial realisation in the simplest terms is better than not making an attempt at all. This is why those who take part in an anthroposophical conference of architects would not like to miss doing eurythmy, which provides the basis of a future training in balance and proportion in movement.

The goal is thus a high one, and the stringent limitations imposed on architectural imagination both from within and without by the character of modern civilisation cannot be thrown off without a struggle. If a contribution has so far been made from the anthroposophical side since Steiner's day, it probably lies more in the concerted overcoming of difficulties and the mutual exploration of the deeper nature of the task than in any specific solution or superlative example. This fact—the development of a new art of finding out what happens in various human situations as a basis for a truly practical architectural solution—dare not be overlooked. The real work, leading to responsible and economic solutions, often begins where discussion is commonly broken off. It is a matter of finding, not wasting time.

*   *   *

Have the situation and the process that have been described an inner meaning that is not apparent on the surface? From the artist's point of view, No! because the whole technical process only exists in order to produce the visible result, like the painting on the wall. Yet the colour can have depth, and in this sense architecture's contribution to life can be of the profoundest significance for good, because you cannot get away from its influence. This is why Rudolf Steiner devoted so much energy and care in its pursuit and renewal. He had some bitter words to say about certain trends, but never in a negative spirit. His sole aim was to set a positive example and to encourage others in the unfoldment of their own powers. He showed that there is such a

thing as architectural imagination that can spring, fully
armed like Athene, from the head of man, if he only find the
means of setting it free. It must be all too obvious that this
faculty of thinking in building forms has become atrophied.
All the more credit must go to men like Louis Sullivan,
Frank Lloyd Wright, Antoni Gaudi, Le Corbusier, Erich
Mendelsohn, Eero Saarinen, who began to wrest themselves
from the prison house. Becoming 'fancy free' does not mean
becoming irresponsible or losing one's grip on reality. On the
contrary, it means recognising more fully one's social responsibility.

In describing the greatest architectural achievements of
the past, in Egypt, Greece and the Middle Ages, Emerson
exclaims:

> For, out of thought's interior sphere
> these wonders rose to upper air.

And one may ask, has the supply of 'wonders' been exhausted? Or has man's structural mind something in store
which only the present and future are capable of appreciat-
ing and for which they are yearning?

The new architectural image-building power is able,
systematically trained, to become 'exact phantasy', a
precise artistic instrument in the hands of the moulding and
shaping architect and designer. Only the individual so
equipped will be able to work in the true interests of the
community.

Our age has seen a vast increase in the range of architectural tasks. Compare it with the limited keyboard of the
Middle Ages. Yet the prototypes that were then found for
ecclesiastic, monastic, administrative, royal, mercantile,
patrician, defence, agricultural and other building tasks,
like variations on a theme, were never monotonous, and
helped to give varying human existences a sense of common
purpose and meaning. Now that man and his concerns have
come to mean more to man than ever before, an even greater

73

responsibility devolves upon the architect, the planner, the engineer, the designer, the sculptor, the painter, the educator —and the industrialist and economist—to co-operate as never before, learning from each other and from representatives of the community at large, which they must consult as equal partners before it is too late.

It cannot help to give meaning to existence if it is made difficult to distinguish a hospital from an administrative block, or a nursery school from a travel bureau, and if certain activities are chiefly recognisable by the excruciating architectural ugliness in which they have to be pursued. There is no time to lose, but there is no lack of encouragement. It is a matter of working to find prototypes for buildings ranging from centres of spiritual activity to extensive industrial plant. Small beginnings can lead to greater things. It is fair to say that the new premises of Steiner schools look and feel like schools, whilst showing no lack of variety. Colour is frequently employed as a major factor in the design, and new techniques of application are constantly being improved. If the search for valid solutions in a realm for which there has hitherto been no prototype has met with some success, there is hope that it should be possible to advance from the vantage ground gained particularly in the educational sphere on to further potential architectural fields that have so far lain fallow.

It is a matter of primary importance to enter the realm of industry and commerce with architectural organising sense and shaping power. This was the sphere Steiner was aiming at (see his *The Social Future*, 1919).* The very building which has been the least understood among his own architectural works—the famous 'Heizhaus' for the central heating plant at Dornach—is the one which best illustrates the nature of the task of housing the products of technology. Where oppor-

* Rudolf Steiner, *The Social Future* (Anthroposophic Press Inc., N.Y., 1972)

tunity has presented itself, architects who are convinced of the relevance of Steiner's aim of *showing what processes are going on through the shape and character of the architectural shell*, have sought to work with this principle and have always felt they have at least inched along the right track in making the attempt. Much more must be done.

This brief report on a chapter of architecture during the past fifty years shall end on this note of stressing the importance of industrial building, even though a new impulse must always start with education. It would not be difficult to show that Rudolf Steiner was one of the chief protagonists of the art of building as a benefactor to the community. Architectural authors who have made this discovery in recent years have already published their observations in the journals and in books that have enjoyed a wide circulation. Chief among them are Dennis Sharp in the West, Wolfgang Pehnt in Central Europe and Kenji Imai in the East. 'Walls will begin to speak', Steiner said, and he illustrated this possibility in the first Goetheanum—which he called the 'House of Speech'. He showed a way in which architecture can find a language that will infuse peace and harmony into human souls, and thereby realise its true social function.

Steiner school building schemes referred to on p. 64.

Kirstofferskola, Bromma/Stockholm. Architect: Eric Asmussen.

Green Meadow School, Spring Valley, N.Y. Architect: Walter Leicht.

Toronto Waldorf School. Architect and project manager: Denis Bowman.

Michel Hall, Forest Row, Sussex. Architects of recent work: Barbara and Denis Devaris.

Rudolf Steiner Schule, Basle. Architect: H. F. Leu.

Hibernia Schule, Wanne-Eickel. Architect: Gundolf Bocke-
mühl.

Rudolf Steiner Schule, Bochum-Langendreer. Architect:
Werner Seyfert.

Freie Waldorfschule, Heidenheim (under construction)
Architect: Werner Seyfert.

Freie Waldorfschule, Kassel-Wilhelmshöhe. Architects: Prof.
L. H. Kresse and Rex Raab.

Freie Waldorfschule, Engelberg. Architects: Rex Raab and
Christian Klein.

FURTHER READING

Rudolf Steiner, *Ways to a New Style in Architecture* (Anthroposophical Publishing Co., London, 1927)

Dennis Sharp, *Modern Architecture and Expressionism* (Long-
mans, 1966)

Wolfgang Pehnt, *Expressionist Architecture* (Thames and
Hudson, 1973)

Ed. A. C. Harwood, *The Faithful Thinker* (Hodder and
Stoughton, 1961). Article on Rudolf Steiner's architecture
by K. Bayes.

5. EDUCATION

The Normal Child

by EILEEN HUTCHINS

Fifty years have passed since the founding of the first Rudolf Steiner School in England.* During this time the Waldorf School educational movement has grown so phenomenally that there are now more than 100 schools spread over Northern and Western Europe and the English speaking world.

The problems which Rudolf Steiner foresaw half a century ago have become far more acute, and destructive influences, which no one could then have thought possible, have reached immeasurable proportions. In the shadow of these we need to consider how far the educational ideals have been realised and whether they are still able to meet the challenge of our time.

On the continent the movement has made a great impact, and schools in Holland, Germany and Switzerland have received a good deal of civic or state support. Many have been able to design their own buildings in an impressive style of architecture, following the indications given by Rudolf Steiner. In the leading schools, where the numbers have risen to well over a thousand, there are long waiting lists for entry so that parallel classes have had to be formed,

* The New School in Streatham, London, since re-named Michael Hall and now in Forest Row, Sussex

and it is difficult to find enough teachers with suitable ability either in width of knowledge or understanding of children.

The quality of pupils passing on to universities, apprenticeships or different careers, has been widely recognised, and not only the original school in Stuttgart but also the eleven others in Baden-Würtemberg have won the right not only to follow their own curriculum but also to set their own schoolleaving examinations.

In England the situation has been far less encouraging. The English are by nature lovers of tradition so that unusual educational ideas have in the past been regarded with suspicion; and, although many of Rudolf Steiner's ideas, which seemed revolutionary fifty years ago, are now recognised as sound, there is no widespread interest in the underlying principles of Waldorf education. No state support has ever been forthcoming and, though some schools have received recognition, this has not brought any financial aid.

Through lack of capital the English schools, with one exception, have had to build up their work in Victorian mansions or stately homes no longer suitable for family life. Then as the school has grown in numbers new buildings have been added so that there has been no consistent architectural design. The running of the school has had to depend on fees, and in most cases, owing to insufficient funds, it has not been possible to pay teachers on a level with those in the state schools.

One advantage in England is that hitherto there has been no law, as in Holland and Germany, demanding that all teachers must have recognised qualifications. Hence it is possible to engage some who for one reason or another have not passed through a University or Training College, but who from natural ability or life experience have a more lively understanding of children and a more imaginative approach than many intellectuals.

Whereas on the continent numbers of parents, who are not

78

necessarily supporters of Rudolf Steiner's philosophy, have recognised that his educational ideas are far in advance of those advocated in state schools, in England up till now it has been difficult to arouse much interest. There has been a general impression that any child who is capable and well-balanced should share the general educational pattern of his time. Only those who have obvious difficulties in temperament, health, or ability to learn, need the advantages of a Steiner education. Whereas in reality the very qualities which help disturbed children are those which are most needed by pupils who are intellectually bright. Under these conditions the homes for backward, maladjusted or delinquent children have flourished and are given state support.

On account of the difficulties described above there are at present only six schools in Great Britain which have been able to develop the education up to the school-leaving age. There are also two smaller ones with hopes of expanding and there is a number of kindergartens.

There are, however, encouraging signs for the future. The curriculum and art of teaching in a Rudolf Steiner school are especially able to alleviate the disturbing influences of modern civilisation. The lack of competition, the close relationship between teacher and pupil, and the cultivation of painting, music and crafts, all help to develop poise and confidence. At the same time parents are becoming more and more concerned about the fact that the state allows them no voice in the education of their children. For these reasons the Steiner schools in Britain have considerably increased their numbers during the last years.

At present the whole state educational system is in a critical condition. We have come to a point where teachers are no longer free to teach out of their own initiative; where parents, unless they pay high fees for an independent school, have no choice with regard to their children's schooling; where the majority of students in training colleges are dissatisfied with their courses; and where the state itself cannot financially support what it demands should be done. It is now more important than ever to consider what Waldorf education has to offer and how far the original ideals can be fulfilled.

*   *   *

It was a time of great tragedy for Europe when Rudolf Steiner was asked to give advice for the founding of the first Waldorf School in Stuttgart. In 1919 in the aftermath of the First World War there was everywhere political unrest and economic confusion, and Germany was one of the countries which had suffered most deeply.

Religious and social ideals, which had been effectual in the Middle Ages when man still depended on the authority of the Church and state, were outdated. Since the fifteenth century willingness to accept religious teaching and acknowledge the leadership of an aristocratic hierarchy had steadily declined; and, at a time when the claims of the working classes could no longer be ignored, the right guidance was entirely lacking.

A new form of education was needed to give young people the impulse and the strength to deal with the changing situation. Compulsory schooling, which had been introduced into most countries in Europe, provided only a very limited basic instruction. The high schools, with their competitive intellectual training and their highly specialised forms of sport, catered for the privileged classes. But the changes brought by the Industrial Revolution had created a vast proletariat who could no longer find satisfaction in their work and whose demands were threatening the whole social order.

Rudolf Steiner had repeatedly spoken of the need for a deeper understanding of man himself and of his relationship to the world. When he called together the teachers who were to carry responsibility for the first school, he gave them a new conception of the growing child and its needs.

He showed how during the first seven years the little child is building its own bodily form. At birth it was given the body prepared for it by its parents and gradually this has to be replaced out of its own living forces. It is damaging to the child's health if at this stage it is approached intellectually. It needs its growth powers to build a sturdy frame. It has to explore its surroundings by finding out what its body can do, by balancing, running and climbing. It has to acquire skills in doing up buttons and tying shoe laces. It is learning how to relate itself to the world of space; and when attempts are made to stimulate its intellect the child's forces of growth are disturbed.

Everyone who has dealt with little children comes to realise the strength of will they can exert. Try to take a hammer from a little boy of three or four years old and there will be screams and tantrums; but do something else in front of him and he will at once drop the hammer and imitate the new activity. It used to be the view of stern parents and teachers that the child's will had to be broken, in the same way as a horse is broken in, so that it might learn to obey authority. Today there is a danger of the opposite extreme that the child is left unguided to its own chaotic will impulses.

We have one great help in educating children under seven and that is their power of imitation. The little child gives itself up with its whole being to imitating the doings of grown-ups, not only their outer acts but also their moods and feelings. It is all important that those who look after little ones should be worthy of imitation. Then the child can find its way with confidence into life. Rudolf Steiner spoke of how the teacher needs to have a religious attitude, for it is in reality a priestly office to awaken the child's inborn faculties and guard and foster its unfolding wonder for the world around.

81

In the future we shall need to have increasing care for what is given to the child to imitate. In an urban environment there are very few healthy human activities. The child longs to experience joy in meaningful work, but is surrounded by the movements and sounds of machines. He needs to watch grownups carrying out with skill and patience work which they love; but most tasks in the home are performed with mechanical aids, and the objects in the street which engage his attention are cranes, drills and lorries.

During these years the foundation is laid for later life. One who as a child has been able to imitate what is worthy will as an adult have confidence that the powers for good are stronger than those for evil and this will give him the courage to act freely out of his own moral judgements. A great deal is spoken today about freedom. But freedom is not won by demanding rights and leading mass movements. Only the one who knows why he acts and is willing to stand alone is truly free.

The different stages of the child's growth are marked by physiological changes, by the loss of the first milk teeth between the sixth and seventh year, and by the advent of puberty between the twelfth and fourteenth. During the second stage of development, approximately between the years of seven and fourteen, the growing boy or girl is still unripe for logical thinking. A feeling relationship to the world is now awakening.

The little child experiences himself as part of the world around him, but by the time he has built up his own body, his growth forces become free for other activities. He becomes more aware of his surroundings. He begins to be fully alive to all that appeals to his senses. On the other hand he increasingly feels the need to express his own personality. His moods alternate between delight and disappointment. To harmonise these conflicting states the teacher needs to be an artist.

Children in their first school years form their thoughts in pictures and love to move in rhythmical patterns. To be presented with letters as abstract signs, which have no relationship with the sounds they represent, is a bewildering experience. In the course of history man's earliest non-verbal communications were made by the use of pictures. These gradually became contracted into symbols and finally into letters representing sounds. For young children the first introduction to writing should follow this course. For the child who has painted a snake and become aware of its hissing sound, or who has represented the rising and falling of the waves, the S and the W will not be arbitrary black marks, but will have a living meaning. Numbers and tables can be learned through moving in rhythms, and the playing of ritual games, which require the forming of circles, squares and figures of eight, lays the foundation for the understanding of geometry at a later date.

During this period children need to feel admiration for what is greater and more powerful than themselves. The most wonderful material is at hand in the stories of the Old Testament. Through listening to these, awe and pity are aroused and their own undisciplined feelings are brought under control. Later, as a preparation for history, the legends of the different civilisations can be told. In following the themes of the ancient cultures children are taking the same path as mankind, living through the religious devotion of the ancient Indians, followed by the gradual development of earthly skills with the beginning of agriculture in ancient Persian times and the first writing and massive buildings of Egypt and Chaldea, to culminate in the brilliant civilisations of Greece and Rome. These legends speak in great imaginations of the changing consciousness of man. They illustrate the loss of an old spiritual wisdom as man turned his attention to mastering the outer world. Later, when pupils come to study the history of post-Christian times, they will realise the new impulse that entered the world whereby man can find once more the religious certainty which had been lost.

This is the age when pupils need the support of authority, for they cannot out of themselves know what they are looking for. The theory that the teacher should stand back and allow the child to find out for himself the themes that interest him is now proving its inadequacy. Surrounded by countless books for reference the boy or girl has no idea which can provide the relevant material. A great deal of potted information is supplied without any connecting threads. The teacher has to choose the content that can arouse powerful interest and make a lasting impression. What lives in the relationship between teacher and pupil cannot be supplied by books. Neither can children of this age form stable relationships; they need the presence of their teacher to preserve harmony in the classroom.

It is from their teacher that children learn respect for one another. They see that all members of the class have their accepted place in their teacher's care. One of the chief requirements of a class teacher is that he should bring his pupils to value one another's qualities. From this they derive the conviction, which they will carry into later life, that all human beings have certain rights in the realm of justice.

After puberty young boys and girls become more independent. They show a quite different interest in other people and want to think and act for themselves. The forming of youthful attachments is a sign of their longing for wider social relationships. If all has gone well in their earlier years, this is a time of idealism, of the urge to form communities, or to help the deprived or unfortunate. Boys and girls should share one another's lessons while they are still sensitive to one another's hopes and aims. Then the boys can learn to value the girls' greater tact and resilience and the girls come to rely on the boys' strength and ingenuity.

In preparation for universities today the chief aim is the

training of the intellect. Science subjects especially are presented in a theoretical and abstract way. The required foundation for scientific knowledge is the theory of atomic structure; and this plays a leading part, not because it offers a wider understanding of life but because it prepares pupils for dealing with a machine-directed world.

Yet thinking is the one activity by which man can come to know himself and thereby to understand his surroundings and his fellow human beings. The first approaches to science should be through observation. By contemplating such phenomena as the forming of crystals, the emergence of patterns on the Chladné plate in response to musical sounds, and the eye's creating of complementary colours, the growing boy or girl is moved to wonder at the mysteries of nature. Wonder leads to questioning and the search for answers.

If pupils are led to a study of plant life, not by dissecting and analysing, but by observing the changing appearances of growing and dying and the transforming of substance, then they are no longer using their intelligence as a recording machine, but are living together with the endlessly evolving patterns of life. In this way they can recognise the true quality of thinking which so often passes unrecognised. If a young person is presented with a thought which makes such an impression that he carries it with him through life, it should gradually change. He may find it confirmed by experience and then it will become deeper and richer; or he may find that the form in which it was given does not agree with what he himself discovers, and then he will have to consider it from other viewpoints. Thinking is a living process and it is crippling to teach fixed laws and maxims which will probably be superseded in the following generation. What is given should be able to grow and become transformed.

In conversations with young people it becomes apparent that underlying their dissatisfaction and anxiety is a questioning of the meaning of life, of the problem of evil and the nature of death. No dogmatic answers can satisfy them. But if they are brought to contemplate examples of ancient literature and art, or passages from Tolstoi, Dostoievski or Solzhenitsyn, which are concerned with these very problems, they gain assurance that they have the strength in their own thinking to find the solutions.

Thus through the different stages of childhood and youth pupils are enabled to unfold their own capacities. From healthy imitation in the first years they develop strength of will. Through joy in what they learn under the guidance of a loved teacher, their feelings are enriched and give life to their thinking. During their adolescence they discover the creative quality of thought. Then they can face life with confidence in their own powers.

*   *   *

The arrangement of the timetable in a Waldorf School assists the children's ability to learn. The day is divided according to their capacity for attention and concentration. The first part of the morning is given to those subjects which are more directed towards their thinking. The period between eleven and one o'clock is devoted to subjects involving rhythm and movement, such as languages, singing and eurythmy. The afternoon is the time for art, crafts and gymnastics.

The system of dividing up the day into a number of forty-five minute periods is detrimental to any real concentration. To have to absorb small doses of a number of subjects one after the other leads to a superficial smattering of many themes, but to no deep interest in any. In a Waldorf School the first two hours of the morning are given up to one lesson which is continued each day for about a month. Then the subject is changed. In this way children live deeply into what they are studying; and each lesson follows a pattern. First of all they listen to the content. Then their feelings should be expressed through reciting or painting some aspect of what has been given. Lastly there should be some appeal to the will with writing or drama. In this way all the child's forces are brought into play.

After about a month, or perhaps six weeks in the case of history or geography, the subject is left until the following year. It might appear that all that has been taught will be forgotten. But just as in daily life we need both sleeping and waking, so in the case of cognition we need to absorb with full interest what is given and then allow it to sink into the unconscious. When the subject is continued in the following year it will be revived with all the more zest.

It is the custom in a Rudolf Steiner School for a class teacher to accompany his class throughout the seven- to fourteen-year-old period. In this way he learns to know his class intimately and is able to deal in an imaginative way with those who need special understanding. Children of different temperaments need different treatment. The rest-less energetic child, who is liable to hit out when frustrated, needs to be kept busy with fetching and carrying. One cannot ask him to sit for long periods as quiet as a mouse. The comfortable phlegmatic boy, who loves to sit put and do nothing, will probably be good at fulfilling tasks which have to be done regularly and conscientiously every day. It is no good telling the melancholy little girl who mopes in the corner that she must cheer up; but she will listen to sad stories and love to care for some child who has been hurt. Then there are the children who, like butterflies, flit from one interest to another and have difficulty in attending to anything for long. These are generally anxious to please and their teacher can give many different tasks, all illustrating a common theme, so that something is finally grasped.

Problems of behaviour, like bullying or petty thieving, can better be dealt with by stories which present the children with pictures of their own conduct than by punishments, which generally have a negative effect. And through his close relationship with the children, the teacher can find the right way to build up the kind of conduct he requires.

There is no headmaster. The teachers who are willing to carry full responsibility meet together as a College to determine the educational policy. Financial and administrative affairs may often be dealt with by a small number; but the educational aims are the task of the College. Then each teacher can contribute his own particular gifts and work with the knowledge of the child given by Rudolf Steiner, without being dictated to from above. In discussing together the aims and objectives from many different points of view a deeper understanding can be reached, and through the common striving there is achieved a wider vision than any single individual can contribute. Time and again it is found that when problems are pondered together, particularly with regard to children who cause anxiety, an improvement comes about without any direct action being needed. Positive and creative thoughts can work into actual life. Whenever possible a school doctor works together with the teachers giving guidance in cases where pupils are in need of special help.

*   *   *

The name of 'Free Waldorf School' was given to the first foundation in Stuttgart, and it was Rudolf Steiner's ideal that it should be free of state control and available for children of all classes. Consequently it did not depend on fees from parents. These hopes were not fulfilled. The Rudolf Steiner Schools on the continent have repeatedly had to meet official requirements though they have received, to a greater or lesser degree, financial support. In England the Steiner Schools in general have been left free as far as the teaching is concerned but can get no state aid, hence pupils are drawn almost entirely from families of higher income levels. The whole political and economic climate has made it difficult for the movement to spread as widely as could be wished.

In 1919 Rudolf Steiner urgently drew attention to the need for politics, economics, and cultural life to function separately and develop on their own individual lines. There can be no healthy education when it is controlled by politicians who have no knowledge or experience of teaching. Industry cannot expand when it is the butt of repeatedly changing government policy. It is the task of governments to deal with human and international relationships. There can be no equality as far as inborn abilities, health and character are concerned; but in the realm of justice the commoner has the same rights as the head of state.

Today governments are overwhelmed by economic problems. Inflation and balance of payments dominate the scene. In terms of national prestige higher production seems to be the only answer, whether the goods are actual necessities or not; so stress is laid on the need to train more young people for industry. The wider ideals of education and of public service are being lost under the pressure of preparing the rising generation for a machine-orientated world.

Until the beginning of the century the thought life of Europe stemmed from the culture of Greece, and the old style of authorative teaching with its classical traditions at least instilled conceptions of honour. But the modern ideal of education is success along stereotyped lines. From an early age children are assessed according to their ability to achieve high grades and be moved into 'A' streams, on the assumption that this is the right preparation for a competitive world, whereas the concern of education should rather be the care of the individual human being so that he may find a place in the world where he can be of service. This need not require academic skills. While claiming to give equality of opportunity to all, the large comprehensive schools, with their many streams of ability, are in reality only widening the gap between the intellectually gifted and the slow learners.

In the economic sphere few people understand how labour, production and distribution can be brought to function in a healthy way, for different schools of economics hold quite contradictory views. If pupils in school are asked why people work, they will generally answer that they work for money. If it is pointed out that in time of famine, when no food is available, money is of no value, they will suggest that people work in order to live and support their families. The idea of bartering of goods will be obvious, but they do not at first come to the thought that work should be done because there are human needs.

There is a situation today where in the East thousands of people are starving, while in the West all kinds of utterly useless articles are produced. There are hideous toys, flashy jewellery, and countless other senseless accessories. None of these things is needed, but tastes are stimulated artificially to create the demand. It is hardly surprising that workers, realising the lack of meaning in what they do, should become bitter and disillusioned. On the other hand many producers and distributors, who have built up their concerns to serve the public, find their efforts bedevilled by the interference of governments, the demands of trade unions and the limited understanding of the average citizen who prefers cheapness to quality.

We can see that in all spheres the ideals that were once active have been lost. Especially tragic is the loss of the picture of man which was taught in religious circles but can no longer be accepted in its traditional form. New impulses will have to emerge.

In his Foreword to *The Right Road for Britain* Winston Churchill wrote these words: 'Man is a spiritual creature, advancing on an immortal destiny, and science, politics and economics are good or bad as far as they help or hinder the individual on its eternal journey.'

Today educational psychologists do not use the words 'soul' and 'spirit' in their descriptions of man. The Behaviourists draw most of their conclusions about human responses from experiments with rats. Another school of thought takes its data from the observation of apes. The followers of Piaget study the behaviour of children from a scientific experimental view. But no one except Rudolf Steiner has been able to relate the development of the different powers of thinking, feeling and willing in the growing child; and he alone has indicated how to guide the healthy unfolding of these three soul forces.

There are many educationists who do not acknowledge that man is a 'spiritual creature'. But it becomes increasingly clear that where only material comforts are valued, art and culture decline and the wisdom handed down through the ages ceases to have meaning. No civilisation can last without an inspiring motive. Rudolf Steiner brought a renewed insight to St. Paul's description of man as a being of body, soul and spirit. We can recognise powers of soul in the understanding one human being can awaken in another; in the response to art and music; and in meaningful action. The spirit is the spark of the divine in man which strives to become reunited with the divine in the universe.

No religious dogmas are taught in Waldorf schools, but the pupils are educated in such a way that their thinking and artistic faculties are stimulated to confirm for themselves the truth or illusion in whatever world conceptions they meet.

The young child who has had a loving and well ordered home where he could imitate what was worthy will not only have a strong religious impulse in later years but will also realise the necessity of freedom in all spiritual life. Submission to the dogma of any ideology or political slogan is unworthy of anyone who wishes to stand in the world as a free human being. The school boy or girl who has learned to accept authority in a class where each child was valued for its own individual worth will develop a true sense of equality in the realm of rights. The experience of a teacher as a source of justice and wisdom enables the pupil to recognise the divine in every human being, however limited or faulty he may appear. And the adolescent who is able to carry into adult life the mobility of thinking and the sense of comradeship of his youth will have the quality of compassion for the needs of others which is essential today in the world of economics.

The reader may well consider that these ideals are impossible to attain, that few teachers have the calibre to fulfil what is required and that many pupils are too weak both physically and mentally to develop the desired qualities. The teachers themselves would be only too ready to acknowledge their own shortcomings and failures. But in their very striving something more than outward success is achieved. They are able to learn as much from their pupils as their pupils can from them, and it is this mutual give-and-take which brings growth. It is not the development of the intellect that is their chief concern but the awakening of social qualities. It is rewarding to hear that many Waldorf pupils, gifted or otherwise, are noted for their interest in other people and their ability to fit into any situation.

In conclusion we need to realise how widespread the educational work has become. No other pedagogical movement in the last few centuries can be compared with it, either with regard to the number of countries concerned or to the active collaboration between teachers and parents. Many training centres have been founded and are drawing more and more young people each year. In Great Britain the six leading schools are united in a Fellowship, with regular conferences to discuss the progress of the work. There is also an international 'Bund', where the different countries are represented and where a link is kept with schools throughout the world. These developments give hope that from such a source new impulses may flow to bring order into the present chaos.

The Handicapped Child—Curative Education

by THOMAS J. WEIHS

Man is not a stationary being. He is a being in the becoming. The more he puts himself into the situation of becoming, the more he fulfills his true mission.

RUDOLF STEINER

The term 'Curative Education' is a translation of the German 'Heilpaedagogik', which term itself only appeared in use towards the end of the nineteenth century, and it was not until nearly the middle of the present century that definitions of the terms 'Curative Education' and 'Heilpaedagogik' were attempted.

In his book *Fundamentals towards a Theory of Curative Education*, H. Hanselmann, Professor of Heilpaedagogik in Zurich, wrote: 'Curative Education is the theory of a scientifically orientated grasp of causes and consequences of physical, emotional and mental conditions and modes of behaviour in developmentally handicapped children and adolescents, and their treatment by means of teaching, education and guidance.'

H. Asperger, Professor of Paediatrics and Curative Education at the University of Vienna, writes in an introduction to

93

his book *Curative Education*: 'We shall call Curative Education that science which, on the basis of biologically founded knowledge of pathological child personalities, seeks predominantly paedagogical means to treat intellectual and sensory defects, nervous and emotional disorders in children and adolescents. The right human guidance that accrues from a knowledge of man can, so we believe, fundamentally influence disturbed personalities in a decidedly positive way'. Asperger then postulates five separate fountainheads—*Quellflüsse*—which converge to create the new discipline, Curative Education. They are: Psychiatry, Paediatrics, Psychology, Social Science and Education.

The impulse of Curative Education is of rather recent origin and has sprung from a growing concern about the increasing threats presented by our civilisation to child development.

On the Continent, probably the Napoleonic Wars, and in Britain, the Industrial Revolution, caused, for instance, untold misery to children, and their situation summoned forth men such as Pestalozzi, Don Bosco, founder of the Silesian Order, and Thomas Barnardo, who took up the cause of the child in need of help and care. These three men are appropriate representatives of the social, educational and humanitarian well-springs of Curative Education.

In 1843, N. Seguin published two volumes on *The Moral, Hygienic and Educational Treatment of Idiots*. In them, he described the experience and insight he derived from working in the Department for Mentally Disturbed Children at the Bicêtre Hospital in Paris. Seguin was a pupil of I. M. G. Itard, the otologist who took on the care and education of the so-called 'wild boy of Aveyron', a child who had grown up in the forests of France, presumably nursed and reared by wild animals.

In 1867, H. Maudsley published his book *The Physiology and Pathology of the Mind*, in which he made an attempt to systematise pathological mental development in children. H. Emminghaus's book *Psychological Disturbances in Childhood*, published in 1887, can likewise be regarded as one of the early attempts to gather up and correlate experiences and insights relating to developmental disturbances in childhood.

It is, perhaps, right not only to mention some of the doctors, teachers and social reformers who cultivated and fostered the early impulse of Curative Education, but also some of the children whose destinies made them pioneers of Curative Education as well.

I have already mentioned the Wild Boy of Aveyron, Victor, who was most likely born in 1788 and who died in 1828. He was eleven or twelve years old when he was found in the forests of Aveyron. His partly dramatic and partly tantalisingly slow development was movingly described by I. M. G. Itard in his publications of 1801 and 1806.

In the year of Victor's death, there appeared in Nürnberg, in Germany, a youth of seventeen or eighteen, about whom Dr. Anselm von Feuerbach, a famous lawyer and criminologist, wrote the book: *Caspar Hauser—An Example of a Crime against the Soul of Man*. Caspar was of unknown origin, retarded in development, having obviously been incarcerated in an underground prison since infancy, to begin with, after his sudden appearance, able only to take bread and water and to speak single words, a complete misfit in society, able to sooth vicious animals and who aroused in the people who met him a powerful sense of the good, or violent antagonism.

Partly as a result of Anselm von Feuerbach's published discoveries as to the intrigues in high circles of which Caspar Hauser was a victim, Caspar was stabbed to death by an unknown hand in the small town of Ansbach in Germany in 1833. He was beautifully commemorated by the author, Jakob Wassermann, as the Child of Europe in his historical novel: *Caspar Hauser or the Indolence of the Heart*.

Charles Dickens's *Oliver Twist* may well be regarded as descriptive of the social stream in Curative Education.

The beginnings

By the turn of the century, the initially individual impulses which constituted Curative Education had begun to become institutionalised and taken over by Church, state and science. The brilliant invention of testing intelligence made administrative classifications possible and gave to the developments in special education new impetus. By this time, huge institutions catered for thousands of so-called 'inmates', the churches developing the care, the state institutions more the custodial element in relation to the handicapped.

Among the very many young people who came into contact with Rudolf Steiner's teaching after the First World War, there were three curative teachers who, in the early twenties, were working in one of the few private institutions for handicapped children in Germany. They had become enthused by Rudolf Steiner's ideas of the spiritual nature and potential of man, and felt that this new insight would have to be brought to bear on work with severely retarded children. These three men applied to their work some of the help and advice given to them by Steiner, with whom they had sought an interview, and while their first small successes found a warm and appreciative reception on the part of the nursing and caring staff in the institution in which they were engaged, they soon came into conflict with the more scientifically minded management. They realised the increasing discrepancy between the hopes and idealism engendered in them by their meeting with Rudolf Steiner, and the scope which a custodial attitude towards the handicapped presented.

Despite the extremely bleak economic outlook of the time and without any financial backing, the three men acquired a house in Jena in 1924, and with Rudolf Steiner's moral support, started the first home for 'Children in Need of

Special Care'. Steiner himself suggested this name and undertook, in response to repeated invitations, to visit the new place, to see the children and to give a course of lectures on Curative Education. On June 18th, 1924, Steiner's visit to the Lauenstein in Jena took place, and from June 25th to July 7th, he gave the twelve lectures which constitute his Course on Curative Education.

Steiner had had his own intimate experience in the education of retarded children, having for a time as a young man earned his living by taking on the education of a severely retarded hydrocephalic boy in Vienna. He guided and educated this youngster throughout a number of years and brought about so fundamental a restitution in the boy's condition and capacities that the latter was later able to study medicine and work as a doctor during the First World War. When Rudolf Steiner held his lectures on Curative Education, there were not only nine handicapped children at the Lauenstein, but also a number of severely retarded children under the care, guidance and treatment of Dr. Ita Wegman, Medical Superintendent at the Clinical-Therapeutic Institute at Arlesheim, Switzerland, which Rudolf Steiner and Ita Wegman had founded in collaboration.

Considering the relative brevity of the Lecture Course and the small number of children that could be presented, the width and circumference of the detailed descriptions of developmental handicaps are astounding. Rudolf Steiner opened up fundamental insight into the physical, emotional and spiritual implications of a great variety of conditions as well as giving a host of intimate and detailed advice and suggestions for practical therapy and remedial education.

The Course, however, contains very much more than this. On the basis of his spiritual image of man, Steiner sought to dispel the then still universally held idea of 'primary mental defect'. He showed that what one encounters as a mental, emotional or behavioural defect or pathology in a child is

97

always the outcome of an individuality, in itself intact, having to incorporate into a hereditarily given body which is imperfect or damaged by genetic, traumatic or other environmental circumstances. Hence, it is always the body or the environment which is imperfect, frail or vulnerable, whilst the spiritual entity in a child, which is his individuality, is perfect and absolute, as anything of a spiritual nature by necessity always is. To the extent to which a person begins to experience this spiritual integrity, even in the most severely retarded and handicapped child, completely new and inexhaustable resources of empathy and compassion as well as effective therapeutic and remedial potential open up to those who choose Curative Education as a vocation.

Another equally fundamental, equally new and far-reaching contribution Steiner made in the Course is the following: He stated that the most effective element in diagnostic understanding as well as therapeutic initiative lay in the inner attitude of the curative teacher inasmuch as he is prepared to undertake a path of self-development, accepting himself not as a static being but as a being in the becoming, responsible for his own development, not only to himself, but for the sake of the children entrusted to his care.

Towards the end of the Course, Steiner gathered up his threefold image of man, described earlier in this publication, in pictorial form and showed his listeners how it can be used as a meditative guideline for the development of those inner certainties necessary for a person to undertake his tasks and responsibilities as a curative teacher. Thus, Steiner laid a foundation which allowed his pupils and followers not to require to adhere only to the letter of his teachings, but to derive out of their own self-development, a continuing flow of creative curative deed and an ever-new grasp of curative educational situations.

While, as will be shortly described, a great deal was developed in consequence of Steiner's initial teachings, the therapeutic impetus he gave and indications he presented are by no means exhausted. On the contrary, it must be admitted that the spiritual scientific developments within Curative Education are still only in their beginnings. However, by the early thirties, seven curative educational institutions had been established in Germany, Switzerland and England. By now, in Great Britain alone, there are thirty-three residential Special Schools and Communities for adult handicapped and two day-schools, all of which cater for about 1,600 mentally handicapped children and adults, and in other countries, there are another 146 residential and forty-seven day-provisions which cater for an additional 8,000 souls, so that all over the world, nearly 10,000 children and adults are in the care of Communities and Schools which have sprung from the impulses and initiative Steiner gave to Curative Education in 1924.

The year 1924 was the last in Steiner's active teaching life. During this year, he lectured to diverse professional and non-professional groups three to four times a day. Just before he gave his Course on Curative Education, he had given courses on Agriculture and Medicine. One of the last Courses Rudolf Steiner delivered before he had to retire owing to illness was one on Pastoral Medicine. This Course has astonishing similarities and relationships to the Curative Course and is, in fact, based on like principles, applied in this case not to the process of *in*corporation on the part of an individuality, but to a gradual *ex*-corporation of an individuality from his physical constitution, with its pathological implications. As the Curative Course established a new field between Medicine, Education and the Social Sciences, the Pastoral Medical Course laid the foundation of a new field between Medicine and Religion.

Steiner placed the developing work in the Curative Educational field under the supervision and guidance of Dr. Ita Wegman, as part of the medical work based on his

99

Spiritual Science, and throughout the rest of her life Dr. Wegman gave to Curative Education the utmost support, and helped to bring about the astonishing growth and spread of its field of activity.

Rudolf Steiner Schools for Retarded, Maladjusted and Developmentally Handicapped Children

Over the past four decades, an awareness of the needs of the mentally handicapped has increased throughout the world and notably in Britain. The inadequacy of custodial care in large institutions was beginning to be realised and, under the guidance of the developing behavioural sciences, specific educational provisions for those children who could not cope with ordinary education were being provided. While classification and educational methods based on the assessment of testable intelligence seemed adequate for healthy, normal children with below average intellectual endowment, they did not meet the needs of children who were developmentally handicapped as a result of genetic, traumatic or environmental factors.

Here, a specific field called for Curative Education. As the Curative Movement based on Steiner principles in Britain caters for children, adolescents and adults with the most diverse handicaps and problems, it is not easy to give a comprehensive description of it.

Among the eighteen residential and two day schools which provide for over 1,000 children, in Britain there are six residential schools for maladjusted children, two for severely retarded children and ten residential schools providing specifically for children with a great variety of handicaps and disturbances.

Naturally, the day schools differ considerably from the residential schools, but also among the residential schools there are wide differences, some having features of the English boarding school, such as separate hostel and school arrangements, but many others are structured rather on community-living. In the latter, the children are placed in small groups, sometimes with a considerable age scatter, with a staff member to look after them *quasi in loco parentis*.

All these schools use the educational curriculum devised by Steiner for normal children, which is described in the preceding essay. Children are grouped in classes with their chronological peers, and although consideration is taken of their developmental and physiological differences in capacity even severely retarded children are included in the class-teaching programme, not because it is thought to be the most expedient means for them to learn facts, but because it has been observed that inclusion in class-activities based on this curriculum has a profound and sustained value for a child's physiological, emotional, mental and social development as well as his general maturation. These observations have been borne out by schools which, for their first ten years, had not used the curriculum but only later adopted it, only to witness outstandingly positive results in the maturation and development of the children concerned.

According to Steiner's principles, the educational approach to young children up to the age of seven is essentially based on a child's power of imitation of the models and examples with which he is surrounded, which ideally would engender love, caring, helpfulness, goodness. Intellectual as well as aesthetic arguments are avoided at that age. This early age is essentially the time when a child develops his own powers of initiative and when this initiative has to be imbued with moral values.

Later on, moral values can no longer be fundamentally established in a child and any efforts in this direction are inclined to be experienced by a young school child as dry admonition, because by this time the educational argument has become an aesthetic one; at this stage, a child wants to be active and inventive, to create in colour and tone, and to learn about the world, nature and man in an artistic and aesthetically orientated way.

It is only with the approach of puberty, from the twelfth or thirteenth year, that education ought to begin to make use of intellectual arguments pertaining to the truths and logical interpretations of things, for a child now derives intense satisfaction from an intellectual approach to his mind, because those forces which have been at work building up his physical organism are now set free for intellectual pursuits.

An appreciation of the fine interplay between emotional and intellectual processes, and the processes of physiological development are essential in the educational approach based on Steiner's principles. Therefore, a teacher's efforts towards his children are accompanied in the case of each pupil by the school doctor and psychiatrist. In regular consultation with the school doctor, a child's particular developmental problems are assessed by his teachers, and specific educational and remedial measures are adopted to help children over their developmental hurdles. Many of these measures, particularly those of a more artistic nature, can be included in the daily classwork of the children, especially if the class is small.

A great variety of other therapeutic exercises requires to be carried out individually for and with each child, often under special environmental circumstances. Therapies for specific types of developmental handicap have been developed in the fields of music, colour and painting, play, application of coloured lights, drama and acting both individually as well as in small groups. Equally, a great deal is being done in physiotherapy, water and under-water therapy and the like. As child-development begins basically with the development of movement and then goes over to the development of speech and the use of language, and finally to the development of thinking, movement plays a central part in all therapies.

The most immediate expression of this approach to movement is Curative Eurythmy, which is the use of special
movements as gestures which stem from the same forces
which underlie the formation and function of the internal
organs and which manifest in the developing use of sound
and language in a young child. These movement-exercises
have to be based on an accurate differential diagnosis of the
organic, functional and psychological disturbances in a
child, and can, therefore, be prescribed only by a physician
trained in the field. The rhythmic use of the gestures and
movements constituting Curative Eurythmy can stimulate
and harmonise organic functions as well as retarded or
deviated developmental processes.

Because the school curriculum devised by Steiner is based
on child development, it can be used out of its normal context to mitigate retardation in particular fields of development in an individual child, so that subject-matter that
would normally pertain to a younger age can be introduced
in a particular group of children or to a child at a later age
as well as vice versa to stimulate certain phases of development, both intellectually as well as physiologically.

However, the curriculum is perhaps less central in Curative Education than it is in the education of the healthy,
normal child. In the field of Curative Education, the personal attitude of the teacher to the children in his care plays
a more fundamental part than the actual methods he applies. Out of a profound experience of empathy and compassion and a deepened understanding of a child's problems,
a curative teacher attempts to meet a child's specific frailty
in complementing it in his own inner attitude as well as
behaviour.

Steiner demonstrated in many examples a basic therapeutic principle, which is for a teacher or therapist first to
realise and accept a child's peculiar frailty and then present
its opposite picture. For instance, with a child who has

fundamental difficulties in telling the truth, who cannot distinguish his own fantasies from reality at an age when such a distinction should have been acquired, a teacher will tell tales which are vastly exaggerated in vivid and colourful details, with which at first the youngster identifies, especially if the 'hero' inclines to spin yarns himself. In the end, however, the 'hero' is exposed or becomes an object of ridicule and the young listener is given an opportunity of self-realisation in a morally positive and constructive way.

This method of creating opposites is not only applied to telling stories; it can and should become a process within a teacher himself, even if he does not put it into words. He must continuously absorb into himself the disabilities or frailties he discerns in a child and reflect back to the child that harmony and fulfilment he desires the child to achieve. Under this primary therapeutic condition, every educational and therapeutic measure will attain a degree of reality and effectiveness that is otherwise impossible.

*　　*　　*

A feature peculiar to all Rudolf Steiner residential schools, whether they provide for maladjusted, retarded or multiply handicapped children, is the rhythm structure of the day, the week, the term and the entire year. It has frequently been remarked upon how profoundly and positively very disturbed children change and improve within weeks of their being admitted to one of the Curative Homes. This is not due to the immediate results of any of the therapies or medicaments applied, but rather to the children's response to the rhythmic-dynamic structure of life in these schools. As this peculiar structured life plays so primary a part in the Curative Homes based on Rudolf Steiner's indications, it is warrantable to describe it in some detail.

A day often begins in the early morning with music played on the flute, lyre or other instrument by a teacher or group of teachers, and then, after all the children have washed and dressed for breakfast, everyone in the house-community gathers in one of the larger rooms for morning song and verse. As staff and children together form a circle, a complete silence is established before morning song begins. Again, before grace is said at table, the same silence is established; likewise later on, when a class rises to its feet to say 'Good Morning' and to start the school day, as well as at other occasions.

These moments of silence and stillness, which proceed less from an enforced rule than from an inner stillness and calm in house-parent and teacher, are an essential therapeutic factor in the otherwise dynamic course of the day, and it is at all times astonishing to witness the response, even of the most hyper-kinetic children, to these moments. Especially those children whose senses are over-stimulated by the diverse mass-media of today benefit by the rhythmic experience of such moments of serenity.

Staff and children have their meals together and meal-times tend to be family and social occasions with a lively exchange of conversation and mutual assistance. When a meal is concluded in many of the Homes, everyone takes hands and gives thanks for the meal.

This 'sense of occasion' is not only applied to mealtimes, but to all the events of the day. Each lesson, each therapeutic session is ushered in and concluded with a brief moment of silence or reflection, so that the span of a day's work is not a mere series of events strung together, but becomes a plastic, living organism, with discernable and rhythmic moments of inhalation and exhalation, of isolation into the self and integration into the group, of reflection and action.

Children, whether handicapped or not, are naturally gregarious, but all children require moments of solitude, especially in residential homes where they tend to move from

grouping to grouping, in dormitory, house, class or therapeutic session. Within the greater rhythm of the life of a day
in a residential school, a child's personal rhythm must be
recognised and allowed for and his need of solitude secured.

Within the daily classroom situation, there is also a rhythmic-
dynamic structure—a carefully cultivated inter-action between receptive, listening moments and the more outgoing
activities of the class, between sameness, or ritual, and
spontaneity.

It is important that in a residential setting, children have
the experience of 'going to school' and not just moving into
another room in the house for lessons. Likewise, it is important that they 'come home' after school into the home atmosphere of their own unit and dormitory, and that inter-action
between 'home' and 'school' can be experienced.

The evening again is an important time when the day's
activities draw to a conclusion. This is the time for story-
hour, often accompanied by music, and a time in which
house-parent or dormitory-parent can spend a while in
intimate conversation with one or the other child in his own
room, discussing questions of life and death, home situation,
relationships to others and the like. Finally, in the still light
of a candle and often accompanied by lyre, a bedtime
prayer is spoken before sleep.

Not only is each day structured roughly as has been
described, but the week, too, has its own ascending and
descending impetus, culminating in the weekend. In almost
all the Rudolf Steiner Curative Homes, the Sunday services,
originally given by Steiner for normal children in the
Waldorf Schools, are an intrinsic part of the life of the
Homes. These services are non-denominational and are
attended by all the children whatever their own denomina-
tion or religious persuasion may be. The first of the services
is for children up to fourteen years of age, the second for
pupils between fourteen and sixteen, and the last is for pupils

over sixteen, and all are held as lay-services by those teachers appointed to do so. The Sunday services are a significant factor in the life of the Curative Homes based on Steiner's principles because of the overall Christian orientation of his teachings, which holds that the nature of man is essentially spiritual. In a sociotherapeutic context, there must be certain religious forms which provide an opportunity to confirm the innate spirituality of the individual. The Sunday services do just this and are at the same time a focal point for a wide range of religious and meaningful experience in which the seasonal festivals are outstanding landmarks. Thus Martinmas, All Souls and All Saints, Advent with its four Sundays, Christmas, Three Kings Day, Carnival, Lent, Easter and the Passion Week, Ascension, Whitsun, St. John's Day and finally Michaelmas are celebrated as moments of intense artistic and spiritual endeavour and provide the 'ethos' necessary, for children and teachers alike, if a therapeutic approach to those in need is to prove both fundamental as well as comprehensive in relation to the *human being*.

Within such a context, each child becomes rooted in the experience that his own life is not a mere accident, but is part of a meaningful whole in which he can play his own and qualitatively specific part—in his dormitory, his class, in his house-community, but also in the course of the day, the week, the year. This experience is not only healing for the relatively astute, maladjusted child, but also for very disturbed and severely retarded and handicapped children, who are disturbed or handicapped only in relation to their innate *human* Self.

In all the residential Curative Schools, but probably particularly in those which provide for children with a great variety of handicaps and potentials, a powerful and therapeutic factor is the encounter between children with diverse problems, such as that between, for instance, a hyper-active, aggressive, maladjusted child and a child who is frail and physically handicapped, or between a withdrawn, autistic child and a loving, outgoing mongol child. Some of the Curative Homes have developed considerable scope for the expression of these fundamental encounters between children suffering from diverse handicaps, which not only foster each child's social potential, but again allow him to be an active, contributing participant in the general community of a residential school.

The training of handicapped and disturbed adolescents

Among the adolescent units in the Rudolf Steiner Movement for Curative Education in Britain, which together cater for about 150 girls and boys between the ages of sixteen and twenty-four, there are some which provide more especially for maladjusted youngsters, while others provide for more severely handicapped youngsters or for those with a variety of problems, both of retardation as well as developmental disturbance.

While orientation in adolescent centres is directed primarily towards crafts, horticulture and agriculture etcetera, further education as well as artistic activities are also provided. On the whole, the day is structured in much the same rhythmic-dynamic way as in the schools. However, these centres are distinctly not schools, but have a relatively mature and adult atmosphere. Training is provided in various crafts designed not merely to give the adolescent skills and abilities in the particular field. The crafts are chosen equally to support the adolescent's development and maturing process. Pottery may be taught because it fosters the free initiative which can develop more readily with a material which is itself not structured but will completely yield to the forming power to which it is exposed. The particular gesture on the pottery wheel also fosters the listening attitude, the patience of suspense and concentration. It can, therefore, be used in specific therapeutic ways. Similarly, the training on the weaving loom will develop spatial experience in its combination of the left to right activity of the shuttle, the front to back of the comb and the up and down activity of the foot-pedals. Both the choice of material as well as the choice of the movement aspects of the craft can, therefore, be made on a therapeutic basis.

Skill in a particular craft, initiative in choosing material, design and colour, as well as some knowledge of the historical and practical implications of a specific craft are not only supportive to the development of personality in a handicapped or disturbed adolescent, but also invest him with the dignity of being an active member of society.

Communities with handicapped adults

Among the eleven units and communities for mentally handicapped and disturbed adults in Great Britain, which provide for about 450 people, there are again those which have responded to the needs of the more severely handicapped and retarded and which provide a sheltered but dignified life for them in aesthetically and morally beautiful surroundings. In these places, various arts and crafts and other activities are cultivated in recognition of the spiritual-cultural needs of even the most handicapped.

The majority of the larger communities for adults in the Rudolf Steiner Curative Movement are more work-orientated and provide for people with a wide range of handicaps and problems, including both mentally retarded adults as well as mentally disturbed adults suffering perhaps from the after-effects of mental illness.

Our age has more or less successfully and partly justifiably propagated the belief that work is an unpleasant and necessary evil which has to be accepted in order that one may earn one's living. The mitigation of this evil is seen in various modes of entertainment, sport and recreation. For the handicapped person an additional problem is created here, because the standards of leisure, entertainment and recreation today in sophisticated society do not always hold the same value for him as they do for the so-called 'normal' person. But in spite of the fact that most people look upon work today as a means of earning a living, even for healthy people a natural and optimal situation is one in which an individual finds satisfaction in his work.

It is one of the most serious problems of our time that the tremendous technical advancement that marks our century has been used more or less exclusively to make work economically more productive, with a loss of the pleasurability and satisfaction that work had earlier on when technical methods were less efficient. As work is an essential and fundamental element of normal human existence, even a primary right of an individual, it has to be made accessible in an adequate way for the handicapped. Work together with social relationships of all kinds in a meaningful cultural context constitutes a birthright for the handicapped as well as for the normal person. Therefore, the question of the availability and organisation of work and life in village-communities with the handicapped are of paramount importance.

It is interesting to observe that the question of monetary reward in relation to work, if not imposed, is less in the foreground with the mentally retarded and emotionally disturbed, while the element of satisfaction in providing for the needs of others is much more pronounced, as is also the satisfaction that accrues from the work itself.

This might tempt one to think that earlier forms of work and craft in the past would be easier coped with by the handicapped. But crafts are technically difficult and place high demands on the skill, co-ordination and planning ability of a worker, whereas machine work and more particularly work based on a careful division of labour lie much more in the scope of a handicapped person and, if organised both therapeutically and efficiently, open up valuable resources on the part of the handicapped.

If an individual handicapped person in a workshop is aware of the ultimate purpose of the workshop to which he contributes a part, the danger of his relatively mechanical contribution becoming fragmented and meaningless can be constructively avoided. If a production workshop remains fairly small so that each of the different work-processes can be experienced by everyone in the workshop, and the steps from the raw material to the final product are visible, every individual in the workshop will have an experience of responsibility for the whole as well as one of being a necessary part of that whole. Equally, each member of a workshop team is acquainted with the demand to which a particular line of production is a response, as well as the means of dispatch and the sale of the articles produced. Thus each worker knows that, in conjunction with his friends in the workshop, he is doing something to meet the needs of others and can, therefore, experience that he is meaningfully included in society. There is, of course, a considerable added advantage when the articles produced in the village-communities reach a high standard of quality and finish and, where appropriate, aesthetic value. The produce of some of the adult communities in the Rudolf Steiner Curative Movement has become widely known for its high quality as well as exquisiteness and beauty. The great variety of goods produced and marketed ranges from musical instruments to children's toys, furniture, woven materials, pottery, engraved glass and the like.

Yet, work is only a part of the life of the handicapped. Another fundamental part is their social integration in a given context. In an adult community with handicapped, it so easily happens that the community falls into two groups; those who care and those who are cared for. In residential schools for handicapped children, the division between staff and children is a natural one, although there may be a warm cohesion and unity between the two, even to the extent that in some schools staff are addressed by their Christian names. But in communities with handicapped adults, this distinction is for the most part not upheld. It is fully accepted and by no means denied that different members in a community have different potentials, abilities as well as problems, which is, of course, characteristic of any group of human beings. There are differences in intelligence between scientists and ordinary working people, differences of educational background, experience, physical ability and so on. The infinite variety of human propensities are equally displayed in a community with the handicapped. It is, however, not held that one section of the community has different rights from another section of the community. There is rather a basic assumption that *all* members in the community work and strive towards a common goal to the benefit of all and each.

This common goal is perhaps most manifest in the sphere of religion and the Sacraments. In many of the village-communities with handicapped and disturbed adults, the Act of Consecration of Man of the Christian Community, described in this publication in a separate chapter,* is celebrated weekly and the other Sacraments of the Christian Community are given in connection with the inevitable events of birth and death in a living community. It lies in the nature of a religious celebration that it transcends the devisive differences between the handicapped and the so-called normal, because it relates purely to the human-spiritual in each individual. Handicapped and disturbed members of the community will assist in religious events, take on responsibilities for the Chapel, for the vestments of the celebrant, and participate actively according to their personal inclinations.

These village-communities with the handicapped also

* See p. 197.

have a rich social, artistic and cultural life. There are regular study groups for a great variety of subjects, comprising 'villager' and staff alike, regular lectures, concerts, performances of plays or eurythmy and many a social function in which everyone in such a village-community participates from the youngest staff child to the oldest, most venerable villager. Further or adult education also occupies a prominent place in some of the village-communities.

An important aspect of any community today is the economic one. It is likely that the economic factor generally has done more to exclude the handicapped from the wider community than any other. In most institutions, however warm and progressive the management may be, an insurmountable difference remains between the handicapped and the staff, in that the latter earn their living by virtue of the handicapped being incapable of earning an income themselves. This creates a fundamental obstacle to all attempts to build bridges in community-living between handicapped and staff.

This problem, however, is not peculiar only to such special communities; it applies to society in general. As I said earlier in this essay, society has failed to use its technological advancement to make work more pleasurable and fulfilling for people. This is one source of the frequent withdrawal from work on the part of larger or smaller groups of society in strike-situations. The other source of withdrawal is that our society has not yet found a contemporary and adequate way of linking work and productivity to the needs of the individual. The fact that our society stipulates that a man's income be linked to his work-output is inappropriate to our experience of each other as persons. A large portion of our working life is bought and dealt with as a commodity, the relative success of which is considered the prime incentive to work. Thus people today are captives, as it were, of an overriding ideology: a man must work in order to earn his living and our entire wage system is based on that ideology.

The fact, however, that a man must *work* in order to live is not exclusive. A man also *lives* in order to work, and long before the gradual evolution of the present-day wage-system began, man worked out of an inborn incentive to create, to master circumstances, to glorify and emulate his own Maker.

In lectures on social and economic conditions in our time, Rudolf Steiner made a striking statement: The well-being of a group of people working together (he meant in any industrial context) is the greater the less the individual in that group claims the proceeds of his output for himself, and the more they are used to meet the needs of others, which means that his own needs are met by the proceeds of the work-output of his fellow men. Here the question of the proceeds of a man's work and his actual needs are disentangled from one another. Several of the anthroposophical village-communities with handicapped people have adopted this economic principle suggested by Rudolf Steiner as applicable to national and industrial economy if it is to become humanly progressive and conducive both to incentive and human freedom and wellbeing. In several schools and adult communities in the Curative Movement inspired by Rudolf Steiner, no salaries are claimed and there are no fixed hours of work. Individual needs are met in relation to the needs of others, which practice demands a widespread awareness of and responsibility for the economic running of a community on the part of its members.

The Curative Schools derive their income largely from Local Education Authorities, Social Departments or Health Authorities. Some of the village-communities with adults derive their income from the Department of Employment under its Disablement Scheme, (the communities being registered as Sheltered Workshops), from their own workshops and agricultural production, and from charitable activities.

*   *   *

The Rudolf Steiner Movement for Curative Education and the Care of the Handicapped abroad and in Britain has gained ground and has developed, its contribution having been recognised and acknowledged in a society in which social responsibility and therapeutic attitudes have remarkably progressed since the beginning of the century.

At the same time, however, the scientific schools of thought which induce men to try to gain control of the so-called mechanics of pathology are still on the increase. The sciences of genetics and biology on the one hand, and the empiricism of behaviourism on the other combine to reduce, to prevent, the chance of finding the ultimate solution to mental handicap and retardation. The same scientific orientation has been brought to bear on the question of the re-integration of the handicapped into society. Both the prevention of handicap as well as the re-integration of the handicapped are seen as economic questions attainable provided sufficient funds, buildings and man-power are available. The real task of receiving the handicapped into society, of being, living and working with them is not faced.

Rudolf Steiner's Curative Education, which is by no means unscientific, adopts neither Genetics nor Behaviourism; it is humanly and positively orientated and regards human handicap, aberration, disturbance as manifestations of becoming, of growth, of development of human personality and human spirit within the limitations imposed not only by hereditary and environmental circumstances, but also by the progressions or regressions of civilisation upon the individual.

I have often referred to, and should again like to refer to, an idea expressed by the historian, Arnold Toynbee, that in an age in which there is little chance that a culture, particularly when it is global such as ours, can be renewed, rejuvenated by young, uncivilised, new population groups who in former times, conquered old, declining civilisations, new fresh forms of culture may spring up in the so-called eddies of the great onward-flowing stream of civilisation, which are regarded by the advancing population groups as backward or incapable of competition.

It may well be that the anthroposophical communities with handicapped children and adults can be regarded as belonging to those eddies of the main stream of civilisation, which are preparing for new cultural development; in other words that communities with the handicapped may well prove to be well-springs of healing for normal society in times to come. That such an idea is not mere idealism and fancy is perhaps borne out by the fact that ever-increasing numbers of normal young people are attracted to the many Rudolf Steiner Curative Homes and Communities and to the fundamental ideas which underlie Rudolf Steiner's curative approach. Many of these centres run training courses, which are attended to capacity, and it is likely that, every year, hundreds of intelligent, seeking young people and students return into society, having lived, worked, trained in these centres and are becoming the leaven of a new understanding of man.

The Adult—The Need for Re-education

by FRANCIS EDMUNDS

Year after year they come, men and women from many lands, from many walks in life, capable, well qualified by ordinary standards, yet unsatisfied. Something is missing for them. Without it, life remains unreal and incomplete. What is it that is missing? They have come to realise in all their studies that the spiritual is missing. Meaning in life is missing.

Early in the century, Rudolf Steiner predicted a swing away from materialism towards the spirit, a change that would come far more quickly than people might imagine. This we are witnessing now. Movements have arisen offering creeds and practices of one kind or another. A term like yoga was scarcely heard in the West two or three decades ago. Now there are ashrams everywhere. There is also chaotic wandering, communal experimenting, untutored idealism, drug-taking. Through all these bizarre appearances, there is a genuine longing to transcend the physical and reach the spirit.

Among those who apply for entry to Emerson College, or to other centres of adult education and training based on the work of Rudolf Steiner, there are certainly some who have also wandered and had past associations with different movements, perhaps experimented with drugs or with old meditative practices from the East. A deep-lying instinct, a hidden source of wisdom in themselves, has directed them to seek the answers to their problems differently. There is no way of retreating to the past, no turning back to the light of yesterday; a new light has to be born through new disciplines from out of the scientific West.

C. E. M. Joad decades ago summed up the situation as follows: 'Copernicus abolished the primacy of man's planet in the universe. Darwin abolished the primacy of man within his planet, and materialistic psychology abolished the primacy of mind within man.' How can we re-establish recognition of the rightful role of the thinking spirit within man, the rightful role of man as a being within the kingdoms of nature, the rightful role of the destiny-laden earth within the world of the stars? Here lie the tasks for a genuine re-education that can bring meaning to life and under-standing of man's responsibility towards himself and the world around him.

*　　*　　*

Meaning in nature and in human life began to fade with the dawn of modern science. This may sound strange, yet it is true. Galileo gives us the clue when he distinguishes the 'primary and real' properties of bodies—size, motion, number and so on—from qualities such as taste, smell, colour.

'Hence I think that these', he says, '... are nothing else than mere names, but hold their residence solely in the sensitive body; so that if the animal were removed, every such quality would be abolished and annihilated. Nevertheless, as soon as we have imposed names on them, particular and different from those of the other primary and real accidents, we induce ourselves to believe that they also exist just as truly and really as the latter.'

Descartes, the first of the modern philosophers, held the same view. So did Newton. So did the prominent scientists and philosophers with few exceptions since that time down to our day. Thus what came to be known as the primary, the quantitative qualities, so well suited for the mechanics of Galileo, were adopted as the basis for the whole of subsequent science. Further aspects of our experience, in which we sense, feel and appreciate, respond to life in art and religion, and which help shape our ideals and aspirations—all these were set aside as secondary, subjective and of no account in the actual world-process. In fact, the being of man was left out from the beginning. Instead of destiny came the term 'blind fate'. Chance became the ruler of all change, man himself came to be regarded as a mere product of chance.

W. J. N. Sullivan makes the following comment:

The vivid world of the mediaevalist, a world shot through with beauty and instinct with purpose, a world having an intimate relation to his own destiny and an intelligible reason for existing in the light of that destiny, is dismissed as an illusion. It has no objective existence. The real world, as revealed by science, is a world of material particles moving, in accordance with mathematical laws, through space and time.

Eddington characterises the situation further. The qualities with which physics has to deal, such as massiveness, substantiality, extension, duration and the like, he declares are in themselves inscrutable.

> Physics studies not these inscrutable qualities, but pointer readings which we can observe. The readings it is true reflect the fluctuations of the world qualities; but our exact knowledge is of the readings, not of the qualities. The former has as much resemblance to the latter as the telephone number has to a subscriber.

Eddington goes still further in his description of cyclic physics. He was outstanding in his ability to translate abstruse matters into images for the lay mind to grasp. He explains how one term is related to another, to another, to another, all impenetrable to direct experience, and having gone the round we are brought back again to the question, the answer to which Mr. X is supposed to know, namely, What is matter?

> Very well, matter is something that Mr. X knows. Let us see how it goes. This is the potential that was derived from the interval that was measured by the scale that was made from the matter that Mr. X knows: Next question: What is Mr. X?
>
> Well, it happens that physics is not at all anxious to pursue the question, what is Mr. X? It is not disposed to admit that its elaborate structure of a physical universe is 'The House that Jack Built'. It looks upon Mr. X that *knows*—as a rather troublesome tenant who at a late stage of the world's history has come to inhabit a structure which inorganic nature has by slow evolutionary progress continued to build. And so it turns aside from the avenue leading to Mr. X—and closes up its cycle, *leaving him out in the cold*.

Today Mr. X is demanding re-entry into the universe. His own laboured construction of the world will not hold him. He has therefore to make a new beginning or declare himself lost for ever. Never has the state of man been more critical or the choice more acute between the awakening to his own self-dependence in relation to others, and falling subject to unlimited dependence on controls outside him.

The first need is to gain clear cognizance of the dilemma, then only can the work of reconstruction really begin.

*   *   *

Anthroposophy has come into the world to restore the wholeness of man. As a renewing path of knowledge it takes its starting point from man himself. It enables him to discover that everything he finds around him is related to his own being, the beauty of the world no less than its ordered structure. On the other hand, everything he discovers within himself in thought, in feeling and in will, has relevance for the world-process which contains him. It is no accident that in his thinking there lives the ideal of truth, in his feeling the ideal of beauty, in his willing the ideal of goodness. They declare themselves in him as evidences of higher worlds which have engendered him. Such inner truths cannot be measured but they can be experienced: they promote change, awaken insights, and lend a new eloquence to all phenomena.

It is Anthroposophy too which enables man to discover what he owes in a positive sense to scientific materialism. This, by cutting him off from all deeper converse with the world, has left him in moral spiritual isolation alone with himself. It has brought him a heightened awareness of himself, and has awakened in him an urgent need to transcend himself, to reach out beyond himself. A longing seizes him to rediscover the source of his own being. This longing could be compared to that of a new-born infant for his mother. Man does indeed experience himself as a new-born child in face of an unknown world. This is no longer a theory but a driving-force. He needs to grow. Traditional faiths can no longer nourish him. He must grow by his own effort. It is here that the disciplines acquired through science come to his aid. These, with their clarity, their integrity, their objectivity, but now directed inwards, enable him to control, intensify and direct the forces of his inner life towards the rediscovery of himself as a spiritual being within a spiritual universe.

To achieve this, the artist in him must accompany him all the way. Art carries disciplines no less than science, disciplines which are equally exact and exacting. He has to observe within and without clearly, but bringing heart and will into his observation. This is the training for the qualitative man. Truth is beauty, beauty truth, said the poet. He has to rediscover them in their inseparable companionship; then to them is added reverence for things great and small. He is thus enabled to raise his qualitative experience to a new and fully human level of objectivity.

That a given flower has so many petals, say five, is plain to see. All who can count will arrive at the number five, and this has been called objective. That the flower has a collective beauty, a unique quality, is no less objective, with the difference that the appreciation of the observer will be according to the richness or the poverty of his own nature. The exercise of counting ends with the number five. The subject has neither gained nor lost in the process. The growth factor in him remains at rest. As to growth in qualitative perception and appreciation, growth in the beholder, there is no definable limit. It is thus we enter ever more deeply into nature, instead of remaining outside. The immense advances in technology, the proudest achievement of our science of quantity, show no evidence of a comparable advance in human morality. That is perhaps the major problem we must face. We need to arrive at a science of nature inclusive of man in his greatest humanity. It is the possibility of achieving this that Anthroposophy opens up for us.

*　　*　　*

The following are some of the main factors to be considered in setting up an actual programme directed to adult education, or, more properly, re-education.

The starting-point being man, we need to learn to regard man as a universal being. Basic to this is the fact that all men have to raise themselves to the upright; that all men have to learn to walk, to speak, to think; that all men can address themselves as 'I', not by imitation but by an act of intuition arising within them in their early childhood; that all men in possession of their normal faculties can work upon themselves to improve themselves; that all men can communicate with all men, if not in words to begin with, then in intelligible signs; that all men are related in some degree in their striving towards truth, beauty and goodness; all men who are healthy possess some measure of love; all men know the meaning of worship, whether it be of gods, of idols, or of other men; all men can propagate their species, being all of one species; all men experience time and build up an inner life of memories; all men are bounded in their earthly life by birth and death. Multiple differences there are between men and men, as there are multiple differences in the parts of the body, but a first aim is to arrive at a central study of man which is inclusive of all. Man stands for mankind and the differences can be accounted for separately. We are concerned here not with sentiments, but with facts.

Next, man has a history which leads back into pre-history. Prehistoric man has left us a heritage of grand mythologies, pictorial representations which, if adequately studied and understood, tell us in powerful imaginations and from various aspects secrets of the creation of the world and of man within that world. We are led through these imaginations into exalted heights, but we are also led down by way of sagas and heroic tales and symbols and signs to the dawn of actual history. Anthroposophy helps us to understand the great historic epochs leading down to our time, the before and the after of the Christ Event on Golgotha, and how and why we have been led into the dichotomy of our present age. By way of such a descent through history we may recognise the great divergent streams of culture, so that though humanity is one, yet men are vastly differentiated from one another down to the single individuals of society.

At this stage, then, we must enter still more deeply into the nature of the dichotomy previously described. We need to achieve a balance in our studies between the humanities and the sciences, the relationship between man as a creative being, for ever bringing new content to the world he is in, and man as a created being raised through his given faculties above all else in the created world around him. Here art and science really can take hands. The history of art can throw much light on the evolving consciousness of man, the divine working upon him, the divine working within him. The science of evolution can set right the popular notion that man derives his ancestry from an ape society and therefore also from more primitive types; but rather does the Goethean concept come to the fore that it is the greater which accounts for the lesser, that the apes are forms which have fallen by the wayside of evolution while the central path of ascent has been maintained from the beginning.*

Both in history and in science we need to get rid of fusty notions derived from a denial of the qualitative as opposed to the quantitative. Nearly all our notions lead back to Galileo's laws of inertia, that the whole of existence derives from particles in motion. Art can bring imagination into science and new forces of life both into observation and into thinking. Science can bring new disciplines into art, rescuing it from mere subjectivism. All this can be studied, practised, realised, so that the split man of today can become whole again.

We come further to Rudolf Steiner's major discovery of the threefold man; that man is three-centred, not one-centred in the head; that as thinking relates to the brain and nervous system, so the ebb and flow of the life of feeling

* For a fuller discussion, see 'Evolution and the Image of Man' by John Waterman, in *The Faithful Thinker* (Hodder and Stoughton, 1961)

relates in equal measure to the rhythmic-circulatory system, and the life of will, promoting action, relates to the capacities inherent in the limbs in their dependence on the unconscious but all-sustaining and maintaining forces of metabolism. This comprises an exhaustive study, still new of its kind, though it has already been in the world some sixty years. The teaching of the threefold man opens up new and profound possibilities in almost every major aspect of study, in education, in medicine, in agriculture, to name some. Man between the stars above and the earth below, man in the kingdoms of nature, man in himself, man in relation to society, man in relation to the technology he has built up, each study supplements the others towards a total experience.

In addition to such studies, it is essential that there should be regular practice in the arts, for each art is a revelation after its own kind of some particular aspect of the nature of man. Sculpture, for example, is an extension through man's consciousness of the forces that have sculpted him. He could not sing, play or compose music if he were not himself conceived and proportioned musically. The sounds and elements of language, consonants and vowels, resound through him, finding their focus in the larynx—man is shaped by sound. And so with every art, and with the new art of Eurythmy, through which the sounds of language and the tones of music are made visible in movement.

The work in art is supplemented by work in crafts to bring grace and beauty and human value and proportion into the things we handle and use and the furnishings around us—the skills engendered in the process continue to serve as living faculties.

We have touched on elements which contribute to an art of re-education for adults—the enlivening of thought and feeling and will for an ever-deepening apprehension of the nature and the mystery of the human being as he proceeds along his path of destiny through space and time. Destiny, and with it the new modern scientific approach to the understanding of reincarnation, give birth to a quickening sense of responsibility for the very soil beneath our feet, for stone and plant and animal and fellow-man.

This is an age of specialisation. All who come to this course are invited to leave their specialised training behind them for a while. Teachers, doctors, actors, architects, farmers, artists in various spheres, scientists too, meet one another centrally in order together to explore more deeply into the nature of the human being. Thus the first year has been called variously a general rather than a specialised year, a year of reorientation to find one's bearings anew, a foundation year preparing for the renewal of the specialist studies which are to follow.

There then comes a return to specialised fields of work, wherever these can best be pursued, but now each in his own field has an intimate regard for his fellows working in other fields. There is mutual recognition of the all-human reality of many members, one body, each in his special work serving the others in theirs—a community of works moving towards the creation of a living and united order of society. That is the further reach of this endeavour.

FURTHER READING

A. C. Harwood, *The Way of a Child* (Rudolf Steiner Press, London, 1967)

A. C. Harwood, *The Recovery of Man in Childhood* (Hodder and Stoughton, 1958)

F. Edmunds, Rudolf Steiner's *Gift to Education—The Waldorf Schools* (Rudolf Steiner Press, London, 1975)

E. Frommer, *Voyage Through Childhood* (Pergamon Press, 1969)

Rudolf Steiner, *The Education of the Child in the Light of Anthroposophy* (Rudolf Steiner Press, London, 1972)

Rudolf Steiner, *The Kingdom of Childhood* (Rudolf Steiner Press, London, 1964)

Rudolf Steiner, *Human Values in Education* (Rudolf Steiner Press, London, 1971)

Rudolf Steiner, *Curative Education* (Rudolf Steiner Press, London, 1972)

T. Weihs, *Children in Need of Special Care* (Souvenir Press, London, 1971)

U. Grahl, *The Exceptional Child. A Way of Life for Mentally Handicapped Children* (Rudolf Steiner Press, London, 1970)

St. Christopher's School, *In Need of Special Care* (St. Christopher's School)

Ed. C. Pietzner, *Aspects of Curative Education* (Aberdeen University Press, 1966)

6. MEDICINE

Extending the Art of Healing

by MICHAEL EVANS

In 1920 Rudolf Steiner gave his first lectures on the special contribution Anthroposophy could make to the progress of medicine. He spoke to a group of doctors who were personally interested in Anthroposophy, and gave numerous suggestions on how illness could be further understood and on a new approach to the selection and use of medicaments.

He was later approached by a group of young doctors and medical students who were not only interested in understanding illness and hearing new therapeutic suggestions but felt the importance of the whole way in which a physician approaches his patients. They also felt the importance of the doctor developing his own personal capacities in order to do this in the right way. In Steiner's lectures to them there is more emphasis on presenting a fuller picture of the human being which could be the basis for new developments in medicine. He also gave a number of meditations for the young doctors to use for their own self-development.

Steiner himself was not a doctor of medicine and for that reason he worked in close association with Ita Wegman and a number of other doctors. Ita Wegman was a Dutch doctor who later founded, at Arlesheim in Switzerland, one of the first clinics to begin to use Steiner's suggestions.

Since then the work has grown: there are now about

twenty-four qualified medical practitioners in the United Kingdom with a special interest in this form of medicine. Most of them work individually both within the National Health Service and privately, either in hospitals or in general practice. Several work together in the Camphill Movement treating mentally handicapped children. Most of their patients are similar to those of any other doctor, but they also, not surprisingly, tend to attract patients who are in sympathy with their outlook.

A group of these doctors, who form the Anthroposophical Medical Association, meet twice a year for weekend conferences. Somewhat longer conferences have recently been started, primarily for young doctors and medical students who wish to explore this approach.

In Germany and Holland there is a very much larger number of general practitioners. There is a large general hospital in the Ruhr where many medical specialists with this interest work together. There are also ten smaller hospitals, including one psychiatric hospital, which use this approach to medicine. In the Netherlands there are two small hospitals and three centres for artistic therapy. Arlesheim has a clinic specialising in the treatment of cancer. Linked to this clinic is a research institute working on a specific medical treatment for cancer and an introductory training course for doctors, lasting three months twice a year.

Doctors working with this approach must all have had an orthodox medical training. This point was always insisted upon by Steiner, because the aim is to complement and develop medicine as it exists rather than to set up an alternative. There is an appreciation of the usefulness of many of the methods and findings of orthodox medicine, albeit at times a critical one.

A distinctive characteristic of the anthroposophical approach to medicine is that it embraces ordinary medicine, but goes further by offering a more comprehensive picture of man. From this wider outlook, a new approach to illness and therapy can be developed.

To appreciate what this outlook entails, some background must first be described. The mode of thinking that underlies most scientific and medical work today sees man for most practical purposes as a superior animal. Attempts are made to gain a closer understanding of his psychological life through the study of animal behaviour. It is also assumed by many that psychology will ultimately be accounted for in terms of brain physiology, with the implication that this will give a more fundamental, more 'real' explanation of psychological phenomena than an explanation in psychological terms.

In biology as a whole there is an attempt to understand complex living organisms—plants, animals, man—in terms of their parts: for example, in terms of their constituent cells. This attempt was introduced into medicine by Virchow in his *Cellular Pathology.** His argument was that man is composed of cells, and therefore, if it were possible to understand pathological processes in cells, human illness would be understood. This fundamental idea still underlies much of the thinking and research in modern pathology.

In all biology, and especially biochemistry, life processes are further reduced to a description in terms of chemical reactions. The methodology used in many of these studies consists of physically breaking up the organism to be studied, analysing the parts, and performing experiments with the parts outside their normal environment. At the basis of all this is the implication that the most fundamental way of understanding human disease processes is to explain them in cellular or better, in chemical or physical terms. Thus the predominant mode of research and form of thinking that underly modern medicine are reductionist.

Although these are the most widely held views and have

* R. Virchow, *Cellular Pathologie*, 1858

5—WA * *

given rise to many useful discoveries, some biologists are beginning to see the shortcomings of a purely reductionist approach. It is in problems related to the origin of the overall forms of organisms that this is most evident.

In any account of life, whether of plant, animal or man, there is the phenomenon of a space in which complex forms arise out of simple forms. This can be observed at a molecular or a macroscopic level, as for example when simple salts from the earth are transformed into the structure of a plant as it grows out of a seed. This apparently contradicts what is taken as a fundamental law in physics, derived from the study of inanimate processes. This law says that the degree of orderliness in a physical system always tends to decrease. This poses the question whether living organisms can ultimately be understood purely in terms of the processes present in the inanimate world.

In addition, living things must be capable of reproduction; this involves the replication of the complex structure of the organism. It has been assumed that this new form is determined by genetic material, with some influence from the physical environment. Although theories exist explaining how the genetic material forms a pattern for the synthesis of proteins, the way in which a variety of possible proteins could build themselves into the enormous complexity of differentiated form is not known. It is now doubted whether the genetic material, as now known, could contain the amount of information required to describe the structure, let alone describe and control the process of developing the structure through the many intermediary forms.*

It is often forgotten that not only are living organisms extremely complex in structure, but their structures are constantly changing in a number of different ways. The overall form of the organism goes through a multiplicity of

* C. H. Waddington, *The Basic Ideas of Biology. Towards a Theoretical Biology*, p. 1 (I.U.B.S. & Edinburgh University Press, 1968)

changes, particularly during the embryonic period. For some animals their life cycle includes two or more entirely different forms, as for example the butterfly developing from the caterpillar. The form of the organism's organs and cells also changes and develops. The pattern of these changes is constant for the species and is laid down as fixedly as the form at any given moment. The atoms making up the cells are themselves constantly being replaced. To the extent that atoms can still be thought of as constituting the basic substance of a material object, this substance is totally changed from one point in time to another, even though the overall form may have changed very little. The overall form remains relatively constant, while the substance of which it is composed changes. In spite of these vast changes, a structural and functional harmony is maintained between the various changing parts of the organism. Although the detailed dynamics of form of most organisms have not yet been adequately described, it is clear that living organisms have a complex form in time, as well as in space. The organism we see before us is thus a manifestation of the processes of this organisation in time.

In view of the underlying assumptions and mode of thinking termed reductionism, it is natural that an attempt should be made to explain the phenomena described above in terms of individual cell-processes and the properties of the genetic material within them. So far, this can do no more than explain some aspects of the structure of protein molecules. The question arises whether such an approach, which limits itself to explanations of wholes in terms of their parts, is capable of dealing with these problems.

Steiner claimed that a science limited to what was perceptible by the physical senses and using only analytical thinking would not be capable of understanding these fundamental life processes. One medical thinker who also found this reductionist way of thinking inadequate was D. W. Smithers

(Professor of Radio-Therapy at the University of London). He stated that it was as impossible to deduce the form of the human being from a study of the properties of his individual cells as it would be to deduce the rules of a game of billiards from the study of the properties of individual billiard balls.*

From his study of cancer, Smithers suggested that the cells in a tumour are acting quite normally *from a cell's point of view* as they multiply to produce an amorphous mass of less differentiated cells, rather as cells do in a test-tube. It is as if cells in cancer show us what forms arise out of purely cellular processes and so lead to the question, 'Whence does the normal form arise?' Smithers suggests that the form arises from 'immaterial controlling forces without which no living organism can exist'.

In describing these immaterial controlling forces, or body of formative forces, as he called them, Steiner recognises that the processes of living organisms cannot be reduced to cellular or physico-chemical processes without losing sight of their essential characteristics. He also points out that a different type of thinking—more imaginative in quality, and yet exact—would be needed to reach an understanding of these forces.

Steiner describes how these formative processes work particularly in the liquid and watery media of living organisms; how they influence the processes of growth and the production of forms; how they work differently in different parts of the body and how they are involved in the processes of illness and restoration to health. He also describes how these formative processes in a plant are influenced by planetary movements, and in man how they are influ-

* He wrote that biological organisation 'is an autonomous process working with cells in whole organisms, as billiards is a game in its own right played with billiard balls, where the laws governing the game cannot ultimately be reduced to the laws governing the balls alone. D. W. Smithers, *Cancer—an Attack on Cytologism* (*The Lancet*, March 10th, 1962)

enced by the higher elements of his being. Steiner was able to give these accounts through his command of higher faculties of perception. Doctors who at present lack these faculties may come to feel the necessity for such a concept as the body of formative forces from an observation of living phenomena and a perception of the one sidedness of a reductionist view of life. They use a less analytic form of thinking to get a clearer picture of these forces. They try to look at the phenomena without preconceived ideas and to allow the feelings produced to grow and enter into the thoughts which emerge. This requires a development of an inward 'scientific objectivity' in the realm of one's thoughts and feelings, if one is not to be misled. The aim is not to arrive at a definition that deadens the experience but to create a picture which maintains a link with the feelings and experience produced by the phenomena. The doctor is thus using his own feelings and thoughts as an instrument of perception, as well as his normal sense-perceptions.

In addition to this different way of thinking, several workers in this field have developed experimental techniques which yield a pictorial representation of the activity of the formative processes in the organism. These techniques have to some extent confirmed the characteristics of these forces as described by Steiner. They have been used in the study of plants for medicinal purposes and in the development of diagnostic tests.*

* One of these techniques, called capilliary dynamolysis, involves the qualitative study of the two-dimensional forms produced when juice from an organism—e.g. plant sap—is allowed to pass up a strip of filter paper. The juices are stained with simple metal salts, a method developed by L. Kolisko (*Agriculture for Tomorrow*, p. 166, Kolisko Archive, 1939). It is held that the forms brought out on the filter paper are related to the activity of the formative processes in the organism. It has been repeatedly demonstrated that different characteristic forms occur at different stages of the plant's life-cycle and at different times of day. It has also been shown that these forms vary according to the planetary constella-tions. (A. Fyfe, *Moon and Plant*, Society for Cancer Research, Arlesheim,

Thus Steiner gives a different understanding of the nature of life, and complements the one-sided knowledge of living things gained through a reductionist natural science. From this one can proceed to a study of the other aspects of the human being.

In addition to being a living organism, like the plants, Man has an inner life of feelings and drives, and he experiences the world through his senses. In this realm of emotions, passions and instincts, he has a relation with the animals. It is from this sphere that many illnesses arise, as is being increasingly recognised by the study of psychosomatic ailments. Although these experiences are closely related to and dependent upon the processes of the living body, they, too, cannot be ultimately reduced to these physical or life-processes without an understanding of their essential nature being lost.

As well as having an emotional life and sense experience, Man is conscious of himself as a thinking being and is thus an 'I'. He can therefore be described as possessing an ego through which he distinguishes between himself and the world, self and not self. Through his 'I' he is able to stand back from his emotions, drives and thoughts and allow his thoughts to influence his behaviour. Here he distinguishes himself from the animals.

1968). This technique is currently being used to find the optimum time for harvesting certain plants for medicinal use.

Another technique, using crystallisation pictures, involves the study of the patterns produced as a simple salt slowly crystallises in company with the plant sap or other biological material also present in the solution. It has been demonstrated (O. Selawry, *Die Kupferchloridkristallisation in Naturwissenschaft und Medizin*, Verlag G. Fisher, Stuttgart, 1957; E. Pfeiffer, *Sensitive Crystallization Processes and Demonstration of Formative Forces in the Blood*, Verlag Emil Weises Buchhandlung, Dresden, 1936) that minute quantities of biological material can radically alter the crystallisation pattern. This has been used as a method of studying the formative forces in plants and human beings. It has also been developed as a diagnostic tool.

Although these latter experiences are primal experiences for all human beings, they are lost sight of if it is assumed that only what is perceived through the physical senses can be a basis for knowledge.

Thus Steiner offers a fourfold picture of man. To the concept of man as physical body, he adds the concept of man as a living organism possessing a body of formative forces (termed the 'etheric' body); man as a sentient being experiencing an inner life of emotions and drives (and so possessing what Steiner calls an 'astral' body); and man as a being conscious of himself (and so possessing an Ego or 'I'). These four aspects are portrayed as distinct, though interrelating, and none is reducible to the laws of another. It is in terms of these four sets of activities and their particular modes of inter-relation in a sick person that the doctor seeks to understand an illness.

This fourfold picture has been further elaborated by Steiner and by doctors using this approach. The different relationships between these four activities in various organs and systems of the body have been described, as well as some of the changes that occur in specific illnesses. It is felt by the present writer that this approach provides a framework, amplifying that of ordinary medicine, into which the various emotional and physical elements of a disease-process can be fitted and further understood.

*　　　*　　　*

It may be useful to look at an example of how a doctor interested in Steiner's suggestions might try to develop his understanding of a particular disease. First, he would study the disease as it is normally described, together with cases he has seen. Stimulated by Steiner's indications he might then approach the disease phenomena with the form of thinking described above to see if he could himself make sense of Steiner's indications.

The following is an example of one G.P.'s way of doing this: His study of orthodox medicine tells him that Graves's Disease is a syndrome involving symptoms of irritability, weight loss and increased appetite. Typical physical signs on examining the patient might include goitre (swollen thyroid gland), warm moist skin, a fine tremor of outstretched fingers, a fast pulse and undue fidgetiness. There are several eye signs, the main one being a bulging of the eyes called exopthalmos. These features are usually explained by the presence of increased quantities of thyroid hormone, produced by an enlarged, over-active thyroid gland.

The doctor then turns to the phenomena of the disease and allows himself to think about them in a more imaginative manner than usual. The goggle eyes of a patient with Graves's Disease might remind him of an animal made rigid with fear. He may feel that the same force protrudes the eyes and causes the thyroid gland to swell. He gets the feeling that it is as if the patient had lost a friendly mantle, leaving him exposed to his aggressive environment. The patient finds it difficult to make decisions calmly, but reacts to stimuli and impulses with anxiety. He is unable to stand back with equanimity and unable to reflect before acting. He acts in a more reflex way, in a manner nearer to that of an animal. The patient's affective life has become rigid, and, like other patients under great stress, gives the impression that he is unable to relax and breathe out. He may feel driven to work hard, with no let-up from the feelings of anxiety which predominate. The increase in general movement, the fidgetiness, the tremor and fast pulse all seem to belong together and to express a specific state of being.

The doctor then refers to Steiner's writings to see if they can further deepen his understanding of Graves's Disease, and whether his own clinical impressions can help him to interpret Steiner's statements on the subject. In describing Graves's Disease, Steiner says that the emotional or astral life is 'rigid' and dominates the other three aspects of the human being. The Ego or 'I' has lost control of the emotional life. From other references by Steiner to an over-active emotional or astral life, one learns that it is generally destructive to the physical body, but, at the same time, stimulates secretion. This makes a link with the weight loss and the over-secretion of the sweat glands and the thyroid gland in Graves's Disease. The predominance of the emotional life over the Ego means that the individual's relationship with nature is more like that of an animal, i.e. he is absorbed by the external impressions 'with staring eyes' and reacts in a more reflex and instinctive way. This also manifests in the excessive activity and reactivity described.

The indications given by Steiner demand a great deal of effort on the part of the physician if they are to be really understood. When this has been done, as in the manner described above, he will have developed for himself a much more meaningful picture of the illness. This approach is very different from the attempt to explain illness in terms of a chain of physical causes, and to the extent that it sees meaning in symptoms, it is closer to a psycho-analytic interpretation. Through such a picture, the physician should be more able to enter with empathy into the patient's condition, and it gives him the basis for working out therapies. For him, this is a quite different experience from that of trying to make sense of the apparently disconnected signs and symptoms of many diseases, as they are commonly described. Out of this extended picture of a human being and his illness comes a new approach to the selection and development of medical therapies.

*   *   *

Many medicines derive from naturally occurring sources—mineral, plant, animal or human. How a substance is selected for medicinal use will depend not only on how a sick human being is understood, but also on what is understood to be the essential nature of the potential medical substance. For example, if the source is a plant, a reductionist approach would consider that the essential thing is the plant's physical and chemical composition. Hence the plant is dissected, macerated, centrifuged, and various other techniques are used to separate its chemical components. When isolated and purified, their physical and chemical properties are studied. Then the compounds are screened for their measurable pharmacological action, animals and other biological experimental models being used. When the chemical's therapeutic and toxic effects on animals have been studied, it may be used in controlled trials with consenting patients, if it seems suitable.

A simplified example of this might be that if a compound was found to reduce blood pressure without producing undue side-effects, it might be used to treat patients with high blood pressure. There might then be attempts to synthesise the compound from chemically simpler substances, if this seemed economically expedient. This indicates the manner in which medicines are most commonly selected today.

On the other hand, one may consider the essential nature of the plant to be connected with its form, the forces and processes which give rise to its form, and the way in which the plant reacts to its environment. One would then study the details of its morphology, its unique life-cycle, and, for example, the way in which it reacts to light and gravity. In studying its life-cycle, for example, one would observe how the first leaves form, and the time and manner in which the blossom and fruit develop. Through this study, and the use of the form of imaginative thinking described above, it is possible to build up a qualitative picture of the plant. This picture can throw light on the essential nature of the plant and on how its formative processes are working, i.e. its gestalt in space and time.

If material from a plant, prepared in such a way as to preserve these processes and formative forces, is introduced into a human being, it could be expected to work on and affect the patient. How the patient was affected would depend largely on the specific nature of the plant and its formative processes, which can be understood by studying the various aspects of plants as outlined above.

Two pharmaceutical firms, the Wala Company and the Weleda Company, are developing and producing medicaments in ways aimed at optimally maintaining these formative processes. The Wala Company has developed various techniques whereby the medicinal substances and their formative processes are preserved without the use of added preservatives such as alcohol.

Medicinal substances are chosen for use in a particular illness by relating the qualitative nature of the substance and its formative processes to the sick patient, seen in terms of his own formative processes and their activity and manifestation in his physical body, as well as their relationship with his emotional life and his individuality or Ego. Again in selecting a medicine, Steiner's suggestions are used as a guide, as well as the practical clinical experience of doctors using these methods.

An example of a disease and its possible treatment which can be further understood through Steiner's work is cancer. The essence of his approach* was to recognise that cancer is not primarily a disease of cells (cf. Smithers) but a disorder of the organising processes. He distinguishes two sets of life-processes: first the upbuilding processes leading to cell multiplication and growth; these are mainly involved with cellular processes and are characterised as more basic (or physical). Secondly, there are processes which are more involved in the differentiation of the cells, the maintenance

* A. Leroi, *The Cell, the Human Organism and Cancer.* (New Knowledge Books, East Grinstead, 1961)

of this differentiation, the limitation of cell multiplication and the production of the overall form of the organism. These higher organising processes are related more strongly to the patient's individuality—i.e. they are more influenced by his 'I' and his life of thought, emotions and drives. In health these two sets of processes are in balance. In cancer the individual's higher organising processes are weaker and the more basic cellular processes predominant. This leads to a proliferation of cells and a loss of form and differentiation which produces a tumour. It follows that treatment should be aimed at strengthening the individual's higher organising processes.

Modern chemotherapy and radiotherapy, which destroy rapidly growing cells, may be thought of as weakening the upbuilding cellular processes. This unfortunately tends to be accompanied by the destruction of many other necessary cells. With careful use these side-effects can be reduced, and along with surgery they remain necessary forms of therapy for many patients.

Through his special faculties of perception, Steiner suggested the use of mistletoe as a plant rich in the higher organising forces. Although it may be difficult to understand this fully, without similar faculties, by studying the phenomena in the manner outlined one can come to a similar picture: The overall form of the mistletoe plant is approximately spherical and lacks the vertical structure that is a feature of most plants. Its form is not influenced by gravity (it lacks geotropism). It has no real root and always grows on trees, never on the ground. All these features suggest a certain independence, and lack of influence by the earth. It carries berries all the year round and flowers in winter, unlike most other plants. Thus its whole organisation in time runs counter to the normal rhythm of most plant life and establishes its own individual rhythm. Thus the whole form of mistletoe in time and space has the theme of its own strong individuality and its independence from earth forces and the rhythms of the seasons. It is the corresponding individualistic formative forces in a cancer patient which require strengthening.

On this basis a mistletoe treatment for cancer, marketed as Iscador, has been prepared and is being further developed by the Society for Cancer Research at Arlesheim in Switzerland. There is growing evidence of its effect on tumour size in animals, as well as on their temperature and their immunological systems. There is also evidence suggesting its usefulness as a treatment for cancer patients* although it is certainly not a proven cure. It is prescribed by many individual doctors and used as part of a holistic treatment for cancer patients at a number of clinics in the Netherlands, Germany and Switzerland.

As the formative forces that require strengthening are those most connected with the patient's own individuality and his psychological life, further methods of treatment are being developed which stimulate the patient's individuality to work upon his organising processes in a strengthening manner.

In order that the patient's emotional life shall also work in a constructive manner on his formative processes, a form of painting therapy is used† that brings harmony to the patient's feelings (see below). Steiner indicates that an individual's 'I' works most actively into his formative processes through the medium of warmth. Hot baths are therefore used as part of the treatment. In this context, the recent finding of the efficacy of heat treatment in cancer is of interest.‡ In addition to these physical and artistic therapies,

* M. R. Evans and A. W. Preece, *Viscum album—A possible treatment for Cancer?* (*Bristol Medico-Chirurgical Journal*, vol. 88, 1973, p. 17)

† M. Hauschka, *Painting as an Exercise for Breathing* (*Anthroposophical Quarterly*, vol. 15, no. 3, Autumn 1970, p. 53)

‡ O. Gillie, *Hot wax baths used to aid 'hopeless' cancer victims* (*Sunday Times*, September 22nd, 1974, p. 1)

efforts are made to strengthen the patient's individuality by personal counselling, aimed at helping the patient to come to terms with his illness.

The Lucas Clinic at Arlesheim, Switzerland, specialises in the treatment of cancer patients and is pioneering much of this work. Many of the patients also receive radio-therapy or surgery at other centres. In combining these forms of treatment, a comprehensive treatment programme has been produced which treats the whole patient.

The treatment of cancer illustrates how from an understanding of the interaction of the four aspects of a human being in illness specific medical therapies can be developed.

*　　*　　*

Now that we have an increased understanding of how a patient's emotional life may interact with his life processes to bring about physical illness, there is a need for methods of therapy which can directly affect these activities and bring about a more harmonious relationship between them. For this a variety of the arts has been developed for specifically therapeutic purposes by Steiner and therapists who have valued his suggestions.

Eurythmy, an art of movement created by Steiner, has been used in specific ways for therapy. It has been called 'visible speech', for it strives to find movements which relate to the activity, feeling and gestures of spoken sound. Certain movements and gestures are used for therapeutic purposes. Through the movements the conscious relationship of the individual to his body goes through a variety of changes. The pattern of these changes is felt to alter the relationship between the patient's conscious life and the formative life-processes in his body.

In particular, it may help to loosen what W. Reich called 'character armour', those habitual patterns of movement and posture which the individual takes up in response to his

142

environment. For example, the person who finds his environment somewhat emotionally frightening, may keep his neck muscles tense, his shoulders hunched and his breathing shallow. He can then be given eurythmy exercises in which he first experiences more consciously the contracted posture he habitually adopts and the crampled feelings that tend to accompany it. Such an exercise would involve an almost uncomfortable crossing of the arms and legs and give rise to the experience of being locked in oneself. This might be followed by the exercise of stretching the arms out at the sides in a gesture of wonder. The attempt is not just to do the movements but to be open to the type of feeling that can accompany the gestures. In alternating two such exercises not only is a physical breathing encouraged, but also an 'emotional breathing'. Such exercises are prescribed by the doctor, practised first with a therapist and then done by the patient alone. Through them it would be hoped to give the patient the opportunity of freeing himself from habitual emotional and physical postures which were at the root of the illness.

Other artistic therapies have been developed which have a direct effect on a patient's emotional life, like painting and music therapy. A particular form of painting therapy, by M. Hauschka, is taught at the School for Artistic Therapy at Boll in Southern Germany. One method uses water colours, mainly the primary colours, painted on damp paper. There is less emphasis on catharsis and interpretation than in other forms of art therapy. Instead, the therapist helps the patient to create and experience a harmony in the mixing and painting of the colours. The painting is not rushed. There is time simply to look at the colours, and the patient is encouraged to aim not so much at producing a fine work of art as at enjoying the process itself. Such a therapy might be prescribed for a depressed patient, or one with a rigid, obsessional personality. The latter might be encouraged to concentrate on allowing the colours to blend well with each other, rather than on creating hard lines. It is found that for the patient to experience himself as able to bring about harmonious changes in the colours and in the way he handles them encourages corresponding changes in his inner state. Thus the depressed patient who experiences changes in colour begins to experience changes in his feeling life. Colour and movement are brought into a feeling life that had been monotonously grey.

These techniques of painting therapy are practised in a number of general medical centres on the Continent, where they are used as part of the treatment of physical illness of psychological origin. They are also used at the Lucas Clinic as part of the treatment for cancer. In England there are at present a few therapists trained and practising these methods under the supervision of doctors. A course started in Gloucestershire* provides the first-year of a training in painting therapy which can be completed in Boll.

Artistic therapies such as Eurythmy and painting play a large part in the treatment programme at the Friedrich Huseman Clinic near Freiburg in the Black Forest. This is a psychiatric hospital in which methods of treatment for mental disorders are being developed, based on Steiner's suggestions. As with physical illness, there is an attempt to see the psychological disorder in terms of all four aspects of the human being, as outlined above. Thus, while it might be concluded that an important element in a particular patient's problem was the malfunctioning of an internal organ, requiring treatment, this physical disorder would be seen as only part of the problem, involving not only the patient's physical body and its processes, but also his emotions and experiences, and would probably have a meaning in terms of his biography. A comprehensive treatment might well

* V. G. Taberner, *Two Year Training Course in Artistic Therapy* (Artistic Therapy Centre, Fox Elms House, Tuffley, Gloucester)

involve medical measures aimed primarily at the dis-
ordered life-processes; artistic therapies aimed at harmonis-
ing the affective life; and individual psychotherapy with a
doctor, aimed at helping the individual to sort out some of
his life-problems for himself.

It would be an oversimplification to see the artistic
therapy as affecting only the emotional life. Clay modelling,
for example, besides encouraging self-confidence through the
practical achievement of creating something, can also help
to bring a patient's consciousness more into his body, in this
case particularly into his hands and arms. The patient is
encouraged to model, for example, the platonic solids, using
the whole of his hand rather than the finger-tips. This takes
a long time and involves turning the clay between the hands
and patiently pressing with both hands and arms. The form
emerges out of the movement and force of the arms and is
experienced as such. This exercise could be useful for certain
schizoid and schizophrenic patients, and for others who have
a feeling of unreality where they experience themselves as
alienated from their bodies. The aim here is to encourage a
closer union of the patient's individuality, or 'I' with his
experience of his body and his physical activities.

*   *   *

An awareness of the influence of a patient's emotional life on
the course of his illness leads to a recognition of the importance of the social environment in which he receives his
treatment. Special attention has been paid to this in a large
community general hospital recently built in Herdecke, in
the Ruhr. Here, attempts have been made to humanise
relationships among the staff. The usual hierarchical
system has been modified. This is done by the staff working
as teams and by reducing the vast differences in salaries
between junior and senior doctors that prevails in most
German hospitals. Efforts are made to involve nursing staff

in decisions and there are meetings at which all staff members discuss common problems. By improving the social and human relationships among staff, the relationship between staff and patients can also be improved.

Through these various insights and practical activities a physician can extend his understanding and treatment of patients. But, as was implied, he is also given the challenge to cultivate his own mode of thinking and the possibility of developing his own inner life. Some of the ways of doing this are outlined in Steiner's *Knowledge of the Higher worlds. How is it Achieved?** Certain exercises are given to awaken higher forms of perception, but there are also many exercises concerned with fundamental human capacities, for example the capacity for true listening to another person, such that one refrains from immediately passing judgement on what is being said and enters into the feelings of the speaker. There are also meditations given specifically for doctors in order to strengthen their will to help and heal the patient.

It is well recognised that the physician who inspires confidence, who shows real interest in his patients as people and makes them feel that he wants to help them, has a therapeutic effect in his own right.† Equally with all doctors, the doctor with a special interest in Steiner's work will do all he can to help fight his patient's illness, but, unlike many, he does not see all illness and suffering as meaningless accidents. While treating the patient, he will try to help in such a way that something creative for the individual may emerge from

---

* Rudolf Steiner Press, London, 1969

† Michael Balint in his book, *The Doctor, His Patient and the Illness* (Pitman Medical Publications, London, 1968) indicates that the doctor can be regarded as 'a medicine' himself. He comes to this conclusion after studying the large placebo affect that accompanies the prescription of any medication. He describes how a major part of what a patient is often seeking is someone to listen and show concern. The way a doctor responds to this need can determine the degree to which he can really help the patient with his illness.

the otherwise unpleasant experience of illness. This will vary enormously amongst patients. A patient who bravely faces and overcomes a fearful situation may emerge with added inner strength. For another patient, the experience of an illness may lead to a greater appreciation of life or a reassessment of his previous values. Other illnesses may call for a change of life-style, for example, a slowing down and a need to develop more inward activities in the case of an overactive and over-anxious businessman who has had a series of heart attacks. He may require a considerable amount of support to be able to do this. The importance of supporting a patient emotionally and spiritually is taken very seriously, and it is well-known from clinical observation how the morale of a patient often affects the outcome of his illness.

Many of these things are done intuitively by all good doctors. In medicine influenced by Anthroposophy, the need for them emerges consciously as an integral part of the picture of man with which the physician works. This cannot be said of any form of medicine which rests purely on a mechanical or atomistic conception of man.

*　　*　　*

An entirely new dimension is opened up for the physician by Steiner's treatment of the doctrines of reincarnation and karma. They are not, of course, peculiar to him, but his interpretation of them brings them into close relation with therapy. A doctor who accepts them, or takes them as a working hypothesis, will recognise that in every patient there is an Ego or 'I' which has passed through a series of lives on earth, separated by long periods spent in the spiritual world while the Ego garners the experience of its last life and prepares for its next incarnation. This will be influenced in some measure by the actions performed, the human relationships experienced and the capacities acquired during previous lives. These influences will extend to the choice of parents through whom the Ego will re-enter earthly life and the type of body in which it incarnates.

When a congenital abnormality occurs, ordinary medicine will sometimes attribute it to a definite cause, which may be hereditary or incidental to pregnancy; in any case it will be regarded with sympathy as a meaningless misfortune. In the context of reincarnation, it will be seen as having a possible connection with previous lives. During its sojourn in the spiritual world, where motives and value-judgements will be different from those that normally prevail on earth, the Ego may have resolved to accept a bodily handicap in its next life in order to make good some failure or neglected obligation in a previous life, or perhaps in order to strengthen itself for future lives. Steiner, however, always emphasised that many variations and exceptions can occur, and that only a high degree of seership can discern the origin of afflicting—or favourable—circumstances in the life-pattern of an individual.

The value of these concepts for the doctor is that they help him to look on abnormalities in a much more positive way than is usual in modern medicine. He will take full account of any scientific findings that can throw light on the immediate antecedents of the trouble, but he will not stop there. In a defective or handicapped child he will see, not a piece of faulty machinery to be given whatever care is available until death removes it, but an individual spirit who is dwelling for this span of one life in an imperfect body, undergoing an experience which it may or may not have 'chosen', but which in any case can have meaning and value for its lives to come. This is the view that guides the Rudolf Steiner Homes for 'children in need of special care', and it is partly responsible for the encouraging results they achieve and the high reputation they have earned.

In the case of illness or accident the doctor will have similar thoughts in mind; hence he will take a positive, constructive attitude towards the ailment and will encourage his patients to do the same, in the way outlined above. He will never thrust his ideas on his patients, but those who are apparently seeking something, or who ask about spiritual matters could be told something about Anthroposophy. They could also be offered certain meditative exercises which might help them in the struggle with their illness.

* * *

Thus, to summarize, Steiner gives the doctor a much wider and deeper picture of the patient than could be had from ordinary medicine. A patient, for him, is a being of body, soul and spirit who has the potential for wrestling with his illness and even growing through it. He goes into the part played by emotional life in illness and offers practical artistic forms of therapy for treating this aspect of a patient's problems. In contrast to the attempts to understand the phenomena of life in terms of the laws found in inanimate nature, life processes are understood as being associated with a body of formative forces, an active component of all living organisms. Also to be taken into account are the 'astral' or emotional sphere and the self-conscious centre, the Ego or 'I'.

This picture of the human organism leads to new ways of selecting remedies, with regard paid to the qualitative nature of the processes that have given rise to the remedy's form and the relationship of these processes to the pathological processes in the human being.

Anyone who intends to practise anthroposophical medicine will face an exacting task. He has first to gain an orthodox qualification, and then become a student again. Steiner gave a wealth of medical indications, but they have to be studied and translated into practical procedures, and their implications for therapy explored. And the doctor has to work not only on them, but on himself. In the clinical

situation, face to face with a patient, he will have no con-
venient text books at his elbow and few standard treatments
for specific diseases. Every patient will present him with new
questions, medical and human, and he will have to consider
various factors as already mentioned, which ordinary
medicine leaves out. He will be sustained in all this in
believing that he may be able to do more to help some
patients than ordinary medicine can do, and that these
forms of therapy will contribute something of value to the
medicine of the future.

Anthroposophical medicine should not be regarded as an
alternative or rival to orthodox medicine, but as an extension
of it which is being gradually developed and is still at an
early stage. One can hope that the therapy of the future will
retain all that is best in modern medicine and surgery, but
will have discarded purely mechanistic interpretations of
life and mind. Medical practice, without forfeiting the
enduring virtues of science, could become widely and deeply
human, founded on a true knowledge of man.

FURTHER READING

Rudolf Steiner and Ita Wegman, *Fundamentals of Therapy*
(Rudolf Steiner Press, London, 1967)

Rudolf Steiner, *The Anthroposophical Approach to Medicine*
(Anthroposophical Publishing Co., London, 1951)

Rudolf Steiner, *Spiritual Science and Medicine* (Rudolf Steiner
Press, London, 1975)

W. zur Linden, *Infantile Paralysis (Polio). Its recognition and
Treatment. A guide for the laymen.* (New Knowledge Books,
1961)

W. zur Linden, *A Child is Born. Pregnancy, Birth and First
Childhood* (Rudolf Steiner Press, London, 1973)

7. BIO-DYNAMIC AGRICULTURE

by H. H. KOEPF and C. J. BUDD

Lasting production can be expected only if one continuously restores the productivity of the land. Although man has to mine the earth's treasures and in that way take from nature, there are those who feel that there should be both a giving and a taking. Wanting something new, they consciously turn away from city life. They have a deep, if not always clear, feeling that Nature also needs man. Nature needs people whose primary interest is to build rather than to destroy.

These remarks were made in a conversation among a group of young farmers who met a little while ago at the Goetheanum, Dornach, in Switzerland.* They reflect something of the moral concerns carried by bio-dynamic farmers and gardeners the world over for the past fifty years: the need for responsible use of the means of production; for care in the quality both of the food we produce and of our environment; and the longing to find in their work meaning and purpose that go beyond mere financial rewards.

Today there are bio-dynamic farms, orchards, commercial and private gardens in many countries—in Holland, Austria, Switzerland, Germany, Scandinavia, Great Britain, France, Italy and Greece. They exist in North, South and Central America, as well as in Australia, New Zealand, and some African States. In Germany some 200 to 300 growers are producing under contract and marketing under the 'Demeter' trade-mark, 83 per cent of whom run farms, some including orchards, and the rest of whom are market

* *Bio-Dynamics*, 1973, p. 106 (Published quarterly by the Bio-Dynamic Farming and Gardening Assoc. Inc., U.S.A.)

gardeners. There is also an uncounted number of part-time growers, private gardeners and farms supplying direct to institutions.

Marketing under such trade-marks as 'Demeter' or 'Helios' involves a system of supervision that covers all phases of production, processing and storage, from the building up of living soils to guaranteeing the quality of the product sold in the shop. Marketing in this way originated in the bio-dynamic movement in 1928. In those countries where the Demeter scheme has been fully developed one can now buy guaranteed bread, cereals, flour and grain products; fresh fruit and vegetables, and fruit and vegetable juices; baby foods; tinned goods, meat and sausages, and in some places dairy products. While much of this marketing is on a regional basis, it is also undertaken nationally, and there is a certain amount of international trading. Farms in Mediterranean countries produce rice, grapes and citrus fruit; herbs are grown in Greece; coffee comes from Central America.

At present the number of bio-dynamic farms in Britain is not much over a dozen, and since at least half of them are run to supply related institutions, the amount of bio-dynamic produce available to the public is small. However, in 1974 the Demeter trade-mark was introduced here, and bio-dynamic products will be available in an increasing number of shops.

Many curative homes and similar institutions in various countries, including the village communities of the Camphill Movement in Scotland, offer work in intimate contact with living nature to those who either need training under special care or cannot sustain their lives elsewhere. A number of Waldorf schools have bio-dynamic gardens and include gardening in their curricula. Since 1970 a one-year training course in bio-dynamic farming and gardening has been held at Emerson College, Forest Row, Sussex.

How it all began

All this has grown up since Whitsuntide, 1924, when Rudolf Steiner gave a course of lectures on agriculture at Koberwitz, near Breslau, then part of Germany. For about seven years previously, since 1917, he had been called upon to give renewing impulses in various cultural and economic fields, and in social life as a whole. The Koberwitz lectures were in response to repeated requests from such experienced farmers as E. Stegemann, Count von Keyserlingk, E. Voegels and others. From their work they knew that more emphasis should be given to the quality of seed, feed and food. Ways to halt the decline of quality caused by the new methods of production had to be found.

Rudolf Steiner, speaking out of Spiritual Science, outlined a comprehensive understanding of the conditions necessary for thriving crops and livestock. It was a time when—on the Continent at least—agriculture was carried out on the basis of traditional methods and in the framework of economic structures belonging to the past. Since then a 'conflict of objectives' has developed, rising to vast dimensions and overshadowing all agricultural life. Pressures have been applied to agriculture which are alien to its nature. This can be seen in the way the needs of modern industrial economics and the phenomenon of labour shortage have become peculiar issues to contemporary farming. Rudolf Steiner, although devoting only a few introductory remarks to its economic aspects, made express mention of the need for the social structure of agriculture to emerge from the laws of its biology:

> One cannot speak of Agriculture, not even of the social forms it should assume, unless one first possesses as a foundation a practical acquaintance with the farming job itself. That is to say, unless one really knows what it means to grow mangolds, potatoes and corn. Without this foundation one cannot even speak of the general economic principles which are involved.*

* Rudolf Steiner, *Agriculture*. A course of eight lectures. (Bio-Dynamic Agricultural Assoc., 1974)

The suggestions put forward by Rudolf Steiner were taken up enthusiastically by a group of farmers in connection with the School of Spiritual Science at the Goetheanum. Work began on the making and application of the bio-dynamic preparations (see below); on the making and use of composts; on hedge-planting and environmental improvements; on the use of leguminous crops; mixed cropping and green manuring; on mulching; on the growing of herbs for use in feeds; on farm produced concentrates for livestock, and on a great many other problems of crop and animal husbandry. The joining in the project by a number of large farms gave rise to the possibility of plant breeding, of quality restoration, and of following up suggestions given by Rudolf Steiner for disease, weed and pest control. Thus, much work has been done to improve production methods in diversified farms and gardens. Moreover, the achievement of a right biology in agriculture is a source of great value and fulfilment for those who practise it.

After fifty years' experience it can be said that when bio-dynamic agriculture goes together with normal, sober financial judgement and professional skill, it becomes truly economic. That is just the opposite of the view commonly held by commercial farmers, advisors, scientists and authorities. However, lasting and dependable economic successes are not to be had in today's narrow, technologically designed production schemes with their feverish oscillations of prices and supplies.

The conflict between biology and modern industrial economics is now increasingly recognised, but outside the bio-dynamic movement hardly any efforts are being made to solve it. Witness this quotation from the Ministry of Agriculture's 1970 Report *Modern Farming and the Soil*:

> The Council are fully aware of the economic difficulties of combining modern methods (which are, of course, inevitable) with perfect soil health. Better soil health does, however, lead to greater production

and therefore to better returns. We have tried to show the danger of treating the soil so roughly in one or two years for immediate gain that it will prove disastrously unproductive for several years to come.*

The nature of the bio-dynamic method

The term 'bio-dynamic' is a contraction of the German 'biologisch dynamisch' and points to the method's underlying principles. Theoretical and applied biology seem to be at a turning point. Until recently they were characterised by the analytical-quantitative approach. On the one hand their results are found in everything that bio-chemists, molecular biologists and molecular geneticists have measured or made measurable, and on the other in the many ways of manipulating plant and animal growth and treating weakness and illness through specific measures directed at singled-out targets. In agriculture this has meant, among other things, an increasing use of fertilisers, biocides, growth regulators, feed additives and the rest. Now, however, it is mainly the growing concern about the consequential fast-advancing pollution of the earth which has led to a great emphasis in theoretical and applied biology on the hitherto neglected aspect of the totality which we encounter in living nature. Totality in nature is found on many levels: in the compartmenting of cells as a prerequisite for cell metabolism; in the organisation of tissues and organs; and, at the highest level, in the plant and animal communities of various habitats. In ecology, the biocoenoses constitute totalities in which biologists are taking an increasing interest.

Though the terminology may differ in certain respects, the bio-dynamic methods are based from the outset on a comprehensive study of the interrelationships between living organisms and the processes which make up an ecological system. Conceptually, the method rests on an even higher

* Ministry of Agriculture, Fisheries and Food, *Modern Farming and the Soil*, p. 3 (H.M.S.O. 1970)

order whereby, approaching nature Goetheanistically and using anthroposophical methods of investigation, a scientifically sound penetration is made into the forces and processes which are at work within plants and animals. These are forces which work from the earth but which also proceed from the surrounding universe.

Bio-dynamic farms—and in a somewhat more limited way, the gardens also—are biologically whole, viable entities organised with due attention to:

the natural potential,
the economic needs,
the special interest and capabilities of those who work them.

Compared with the essentially economic motivation of general farming, emphasis is given to the natural conditions under which all life, plants and livestock thrive and develop lasting productivity. Bio-dynamic farms, therefore, are diversified. They grow a variety of plants, maintaining a healthy balance between soil-exhausting and soil-restoring crops. Particular use is made of leguminous plants and 'companion planting', a practice of many gardeners that gives effect to the subtler relationships within the plant kingdom.

The principle at the foundation of bio-dynamic farm organisation is the establishing of closed cycles of substances, as far as possible. The recycling of farm-produced manures is the backbone of the manuring programme. The beneficial effects of these materials on soil-life are in many cases enhanced by composting. In bio-dynamic farming the compost technique has been carefully designed to put to work those conditions which one can learn of from the geographical pattern of nature's humus formations.

Practical experience and the results of long-term field experiments have shown clearly how, in the temperate zones, animal manures are indispensable for lasting soil productivity. (For other, notably warm climates, this does not hold quite so rigorously.) Bio-dynamic farms, therefore, have an appropriate number of animals. In animal husbandry optimum production and good health are stressed, rather than record performances by individual animals. Indigenous herds are bred. This approach contrasts sharply with the specialised animal rearing that has led to poultry, pig and cattle industries and factory farms, where the stock is kept far from the soil that grows their feed and receives their manures.

The measures taken in bio-dynamic farming eliminate a number of diseases, pests and other weaknesses, especially when used in conjunction with all that can be done towards a healthy landscape—such as soil conservation, the provision of shelter for wild-life, the preservation of water supplies, and so on. This makes it possible to dispense with the host of agricultural chemicals which have come into general use. In addition, Rudolf Steiner indicated new possibilities for weed, pest and disease control. However, while positive results have been achieved, the conditions favoured by these procedures are not yet sufficiently understood and more research is needed.

The term 'farm organism' has been coined for the biological unit which is created by such measures and others not mentioned here. In other respects bio-dynamic farming follows generally known sound rules of plant and animal husbandry, but it goes beyond them by putting special emphasis on the concept of the 'farm organism' and by introducing specially prepared plant and mineral substances known as the 'preparations'. Administered in small quantities to plants, soils and manures, they are to be regarded as the bearers of organising forces rather than as the building bricks of the organism. It is to such forces that the term 'dynamic' refers.

The preparations form two groups. (The numbers given to them have no significance.) First, there are two sprays: 500, which enhances soil life and aids root formation, and 501, which is made from quartz and applied to the growing plant. These two preparations are an outcome of a central concept of the bio-dynamic method. All green plants can be seen to unfold their form between two sets of environmental influences of soil-borne or terrestrial forces on the one hand, and, on the other, of cosmic forces that work through the atmosphere. These polar influences are reflected in the morphology and composition of plants. Varying among the species, of course, their effects become manifest in many different ways. Preparation 500 supports the terrestrial forces and 501 the cosmic. Applying these substances is a normal procedure, but their value has been noticed also as correctives of the adverse effects of either too wet or too dry seasons. This is not the place for detailed explanations, but the following table serves to give an idea of what is meant.*

Two Polar Groups of Growth Factors which Influence Yields and Quality

Terrestrial Influences	Cosmic Influences
include among others:	
soil life, soil fertility, water supply, rel. humidity	light, warmth, other climatic conditions and their seasonal and diurnal rhythms
vary locally according to:	
texture of soils, their fertility, organic content, nitrogen content, lime content, water storage capacity, average temperature and rainfall	sunshine, cloudiness, rainfall according to latitude, altitude, aspect etcetera, seasonal weather rhythms, presence of silicious substances
normal influence on crops:	
high yields, protein and ash content	ripening, flavour, keeping quality, viability of seeds

* *Bio-Dynamics*, 1971, p. 97

effects when superabundant naturally or by poor management:

lush growth, subject to diseases and pests, low keeping quality	low yields, strong fragrance, bitter taste, hairy fibrous parts

managerial measures to achieve optimum effects:

liberal manuring with prepared compost, legumes in the rotations, correcting mineral deficiencies, irrigations, saving moisture (mulching), regular use of prep. 500	using very well-ripened compost, no over-fertilising, correcting deficiencies, regular use of 501

The flowers or other organs of certain common plants—yarrow, oak, dandelion, chamomile, stinging nettle and valerian—are used to provide a second group of preparations for application to manures and composts. Although administered by small dosages of only a few parts per million by weight, their beneficial effects have shown up in analytical data of composts, manures and growth.* Cropping, cultivation, manuring and the use of the preparations constitute the major tools of the bio-dynamic method of vegetable production. But one more element should be mentioned.

In making the preparations, definite times of the year are followed, especially seasonal rhythms. This brings in the many rhythmical phenomena in plant and animal growth, physiology and behaviour which are cosmic in origin, being related to, and even coincident with, planetary rhythms. It is well known how the light and warmth rhythms of the sun fashion the agricultural year. But the moon also has known rhythms. Traditional knowledge of this kind has largely become superstitition, but new evidence is gradually showing the importance of moon rhythms for good growth in plants. An example is given below.

Contemporary agriculture tends more and more to

* Koepf, Pettersson and Schaumann, *Biologische Landwirtschaft* (Eugen Ulmer Verlag, Stuttgart, 1974)

narrowed-down production schemes. The remarks made so far show how the bio-dynamic approach takes the opposite direction. Natural ecosystems, though stable and subject to minor losses from their closed cycles of substances, suffer little from disease and pest attacks, but their net production is negligible in terms of human needs. Every form of agriculture, therefore, must change the natural community. In the bio-dynamic method a high net production is not obtained by sacrificing the natural principles of diversification and recycling. These, rather, are enlisted to intensify production. Moreover, the use of the preparations shows how attention is given to life's more subtle influences and to the fact that life processes follow the rhythmical patterns of the surrounding universe.

Research

These methods, derived originally from the indications given by Rudolf Steiner, have been gradually developed and refined by continuing research. This was pioneered by E. E. Pfeiffer, first in Switzerland and later in Holland and Germany. In 1940 Pfeiffer went to America and founded a laboratory at Threefold Farm, Spring Valley, New York, where he stayed until his death in 1961. Thus the movement spread to the West on a larger scale.

Much valuable work has also been done by L. and E. Kolisko, who eventually lived in this country. They produced many results concerning the preparations, cosmic rhythms and so forth.* In the late twenties and the thirties Research Stations began to carry out pot and field experiments, although the development of this work was affected by insufficient understanding of the appropriate methodology.

In Saxonia, a survey carried out in 1936–7 on fifty-five farms of between 25 and 300 acres compared their yields favourably with those of other farms in the district. In central

* L. and E. Kolisko, *Agriculture of Tomorrow* (Kolisko Archive, 1939)

Europe this work was interrupted by the Second World War which caused many farms in the eastern region to change hands. We had to begin again with what was left in the west. The work then expanded quickly. Research facilities were set up and contacts made with institutions and the authorities. Today there are again many well-managed farms and gardens in operation, opening their gates for farm walks in the summer.

The Bio-dynamic Associations and the Experimental Circles in the different countries work together, publishing books and magazines and maintaining research facilities such as the Bio-dynamic Research Institute at Darmstadt in Germany, and a similar one at Järna in Sweden. Courses lasting from one to several weeks are held in many countries. A winter course for gardeners is held at the Anthroposophical Seminar in Järna; the Warmand School in Holland includes bio-dynamic courses in its curriculum. Most countries where the movement is active have full-time consultants; farmers offer each other helpful advice and share their experiences.

In Britain the bio-dynamic movement is still relatively small, but with a steadily increasing membership and a twice-yearly journal, *Star and Furrow*. The substantial work carried out by the Bio-dynamic Agricultural Association, with headquarters at Broome Farm, Clent, Stourbridge, West Midlands, has shown both depth of experience and breadth of understanding. An increasing number of young people in this country, as well as experienced farmers, are taking an active interest in bio-dynamics, though progress is hampered by the problems of land, prices and labour that are causing concern throughout the western world. In this connection efforts are being made to extend anthroposophical concepts into the economic realm, with the aim of developing new social-economic forms which will not start from the assumptions of industrial economics, but will be more suited to the type of balanced economy inherent in agriculture itself.

161

A great many problems have been tackled by bio-dynamic researchers over the years. Brief mention of two may also help to illustrate the bio-dynamic approach.

A major objective of bio-dynamic farming from the outset has been to produce food of high nutritional quality. The nature of this problem calls particularly for appropriate concepts with which to bring many detailed findings into a meaningful whole. Feeding experiments are costly and troublesome, although work has recently been started jointly by the German Bio-Dynamic Institute and the Hanover Veterinary School. Usually one has to rely on analytical findings. To these E. Pfeiffer added the sensitive crystallisation test method* which reveals some of the subtler aspects of quality. Many environmental factors influence quality, which in turn is manifest in many of the properties of a product.

This situation can be dealt with scientifically by using the concepts of terrestrial and cosmic forces, as outlined above. Following this, numerous field experiments have demonstrated how preparations, light and warmth, dryer or more damp conditions, on the one side, and soil-borne influences such as water, manures and soil-life on the other, combine to bring about a certain quality. Quality, then, is expressed in flavour, taste, shelf and storage life, palatability and the content of vitamins, minerals, essential amino-acids and proteins, and, in carbohydrates, protein ratios, enzyme activities, etcetera.

---

* A method applied for a number of diagnostic and research purposes, especially in agriculture and medicine. Essentially it complements conventional analytic methods in that it offers a 'picture' (in the form of a pattern of copper chloride crystals on a glass plate) of forces at work in a sample of soil, blood or other complex substance. See E. Pfeiffer, *Sensitive Crystallization Processes and Demonstration of Formative Forces in the Blood* (Verlag Emil Weises Buchhandlung, Dresden, 1936) and *Formative Forces in Crystallization* (Rudolf Steiner Publishing Co., London, and Anthroposophic Press, U.S.A., 1936)

Vegetables and farm crops, such as potatoes, cereals and fruit, have been used in these trials, which show how composted manures and the bio-dynamic preparations can enhance quality. It is an objective of bio-dynamic farming, therefore, to produce plants which have been grown under balanced conditions of environment and are 'ripened' (using this term with reference not only to seeds and fruits, but also to the maturity of leaf and root). A firm, not too watery tissue and good shelf-life are indicative in this respect. This approach is the basis of the criteria for producing and marketing products under the 'Demeter' trade-mark.* The advisory service uses the results of such experiments to guide and help the growers.

As our second example, it was Maria Thun, who, after twenty years of experimental work, suggested that yields can be markedly affected by paying attention to the sidereal revolution of the moon, not only in sowing and planting, but also as regards cultivation and the repeated application of the silica spray 501. This work has led many farmers and gardeners to take an interest in the use of such rhythmical relationships.

A recently completed doctoral thesis† describes the testing of Maria Thun's suggestions by pot and field experiments. In a manuring and fertilising trial with sugar beet and the application of the silica spray—several times following a rhythmical pattern—produced significantly higher yields in all cases. Cereals responded with less pronounced yield increases. When crops are partially shaded, the silica spray seems to exert a compensatory effect. Experiments with 501 on spring wheat significantly increased the tensile strength of the straw. The sugar content of sugar beet was increased by 0.6–0.8 units. The spray increased slightly the crude protein content in cereals and potato tubers, and improved the taste

* *Bio-Dynamics*, 1970, p. 96 and 1969, pp. 91–2, summarized in *Biologische Landwirtschaft*, op. cit.

† U. Abele, diss., Giessen, 1973

of potatoes. Year-long experiments with spring wheat, oats, and carrots revealed the effects of sidereal moon rhythms, i.e. with respect to the Zodiac. By observing these rhythms in sowing and cultivation, the yields of cereals were influenced, in some cases by a statistically significant margin. The yields of carrots, for example, increased by up to 20 per cent. Weather conditions may interfere with these relationships.

These few remarks point to an exciting new field of investigation into the dynamic effects of substances and cosmic rhythms. It goes without saying that in doing such research one has to steer clear of mere tradition and establish the results independently, on their own conceptual and experimental footing.

Bio-dynamic agriculture adheres to biological principles. Accordingly, farms with mixed production are the rule. This means that the marketing of their food products will be more regional than is usual today, without denying the role of the international food trade. The yields of bio-dynamic farms must be valued in such terms. It is the total output of mixed production that counts for the public. The available statistical evidence shows that bio-dynamic farms produce about average yields. As a rule they do not produce the kind of record yields achieved by specialised farming with just one or the other crop. Here are a few examples. A bio-dynamic farm in the Cologne Basin produced 1.6 t/a of rye compared with the local average of 1.7 t/a, and 1.7 t/a of oats as against a local average of 1.4 t/a. The mean yields of a number of bio-dynamic farms in Holland are set out below, with those of other farms in the area in parentheses.*

Spring Wheat	1.8 (1.6)		Sugar Beet	19.6 (19.0)
Spring Barley	1.7 (1.4)		Mangolds	44.2 (31.8)
Oats	1.9 (1.6)		Beans	1.1 (1.0)
Potatoes	8.8 (14.0)			

* *Bio-Dynamics*, 1974, p. 109

Milk yields are mostly high in bio-dynamic farms, especially in relation to the ration fed. This is an experience reported also by organic farms. Moreover, these yields are produced in such a way that the natural fertility of the soil is preserved and built up. In the long run such cropping systems, in connection with improved breeding and cultivation, will sustain a steady though not spectacular growth in yields. This kind of dependable production and steady upward trend provides an important element of stability.

Placing more emphasis on regionally orientated production means something for the rich countries; it is vital for those of the Third World. They could thus depend largely on local resources and their abundant manpower. Leaving aside for the moment pollution, and political and economic obstructions, the present crisis in energy supplies and in all sorts of raw materials are proof that the Western and Green Revolution type of agriculture does not provide the ultimate answer for the Third World, where the problem of food shortage is most acute. But this applies also to the rich countries. The energy crisis has shown how much energy the national economy could save by using to the full the potential of animal manures, instead of the chemical nitrogen fertilisers that consume the lion's share of our total energy input.*

A similar remark can be made with regard to phosphorus, an indispensable raw material for almost any type of farming and gardening. By making efficient use of the natural soil supply, with a very small amount added by mixing it into the life-processes of farm manures and composts, bio-dynamic farms need to draw from the phosphate deposits of the world only a fraction of the amount needed by other farms.

Biocides of various kinds are not used in bio-dynamic agriculture, except in insignificant amounts. Thus pollution

* *Lebendige Erde*, 1974, 1 (Forschungsring für Biologisch-Dynamische Wirtschaftsweise, Darmstadt)

is reduced. Field and garden crops are grown without chemicals, and there are commercial orchards operating along these lines. It has also been shown recently that the problem of nitrate in drinking water can be avoided by organic and bio-dynamic management.* Bio-dynamic farming helps to improve the quality of our environment.

These various points show that the bio-dynamic approach offers alternatives to problems which modern farming is struggling with. The alternatives do not emerge from theoretical considerations; they are presented by functioning models. These models are relatively few and many adjustments will certainly have to be made as their numbers grow, but as alternatives they are offered by an approach that was not brought about by the problems of the seventies. They originated half a century ago from spiritual insight into the nature of the living kingdoms and man's relationship to them.

In speaking about the scope of the bio-dynamic work we should add that it is having a greater impact on general agriculture than its limited number of farms might suggest. The farms are acting as a stimulant and corrective both to science and to agricultural policy. Their long-continued emphasis on quality, organic methods, conservation and the elimination of questionable chemicals has prompted many farmers and agriculturalists to think again.

The role of bio-dynamic farming in society

An account of the bio-dynamic movement would not be complete if no mention were made of its sociological significance. The following passage comes from the book *Only One Earth*:†

May not the whole development of modern industrialised farming represent a dangerous oversimplification; a trend towards a mono-

* Bio-Dynamics, 1973, p. 108
† B. Ward and R. Dubos, *Only One Earth* (A. Deutsch, 1972)

culture which, being of its very nature more fragile and vulnerable than balanced, complex eco-systems, exposes mankind to the risk of securing high food returns in the shorter run in return for catastrophic risks of famine later on?

In this way two famous authors, Barbara Ward and René Dubos, point to the essential role of agriculture in social life: its responsibility to feed the world. But farming has a responsibility also to long-term economic considerations. Man is in a position now to know that the fantastic growth and rapid returns of agriculture during recent decades have been made possible only by human contrivance aimed at narrow, short-term objectives. The extensive use of agricultural chemicals has led to unwholesome effects on wild life, nutritional quality and soil productivity. It has also made farming dependent on an extravagant use of the diminishing resource of oil. The quest for high yields, coupled with a disregard for the broader, long-term and unseen consequences, has given agriculture a false economic basis.

Lasting soil productivity and the 'farm organism' are more than the central concepts of the bio-dynamic method. They are the foundation of agricultural economics. By obviating the need for artificial substances, the bio-dynamic method enables farms to cut out their cost, an achievement of great economic significance. Oil, seen in a full economic context, belongs to the 'short-term economics' that characterise our recent decades. The demand for oil is increasing beyond possibility of supply; it is only inequitable world distribution that gives the illusion of oil's abundance. A consequence of oil's peculiar economic role is that its price will rise more steeply than the economic processes within agriculture can ever match. The costs of chemical agriculture cannot be met out of farming itself, but must be offset by the sort of massive government aid that in Britain at the moment runs at £300 million a year. Unfortunately, because public financing requires uniform administration, this aid leads to

ill-conceived and generalised agricultural policies and programmes.

The development of agriculture in our time should arise
out of its own needs and nature, and not be determined by
the criteria of public expenditure, industrial economics or
speculative investment. The economic strength of farming is
dependent upon its agricultural strength. By striving for a
more balanced agriculture, and by giving purpose to the
economic self-sufficiency of farms, the bio-dynamic method
helps to make farming economic.

We must always recognise, however, that the grave background issues which concern everyone—the need to feed a
growing world population, to reduce the pollution of our
planet and to use less wastefully our natural resources,
including energy—are not mere technical questions, calling
for merely technical answers. Only responsible action stem-
ming from a spiritual understanding of life and its origin
will help to solve our many problems. That is why the
national groups in the bio-dynamic movement come together
regularly at the Goetheanum School of Spiritual Science in
Dornach in order to deepen the anthroposophical basis of
their work. As with other cultural activities which proceed
from Anthroposophy, the bio-dynamic method entails
constant endeavours to gain a closer understanding of its
underlying spiritual impulse, and of how it can bring a
fruitful influence also into the social realm.

FURTHER READING

Rudolf Steiner, *Agriculture* (Bio-Dynamic Agricultural Assoc.,
    1974)
Star and Furrow, twice yearly publication by the Bio-Dynamic
    Agricultural Assoc.

E. E. Pfeiffer, *Bio-Dynamic Farming. Articles 1942–62* (Bio-Dynamic Farming and Gardening Assoc. Inc., U.S.A.)

E. E. Pfeiffer, *The Pfeiffer Garden Book. Bio-Dynamics in the Home Garden* (Bio-Dynamic Farming and Gardening Assoc. Inc., U.S.A.)

George Corrin, *Handbook on Composting and the Bio-Dynamic Preparations* (Bio-Dynamic Agricultural Assoc., 1960)

G. Grohmann, *The Plant. A guide to understanding its nature* (Rudolf Steiner Press, London, 1974)

H. Philbrick and R. B. Gregg, *Companion Plants* (Stuart and Watkins, London, 1967)

8. HELPING SOCIAL GROWTH

The Work of the NPI

by CHRISTOPHER SCHAEFER

Signs of social crisis are evident at many levels of social life. Spiralling inflation, widespread political instability, and urban blight point the inadequacy of macro-social structures. At the organisational level stagnation and conflict are prevalent while increased violence, heightened divorce rates, and the growing frequency of psychological illness suggest the difficulties individuals have in coping with a rapidly changing technological society.

While the exact causes of these social problems are difficult to pinpoint, a connection between the materialistic striving of modern science and technology and an impoverishment of the human spirit was already recognised by Huxley, Sorokin, Husserl, Malraux and others in the 1930s and 1940s. Today this recognition is more widespread. We appear to have sacrificed the Greek dictum of *Man, know thyself* for an objective knowledge and utilisation of the natural world external to us. As the German scientist and philosopher von Weizäcker stated, 'The belief in science plays the role of the dominant religion in our time. But the key which we have therefore lost is the key to the being of man.'* It was with the aim of supplying a new key to the nature of man that Rudolf

---

* Fr. von Weizäcker, cited in Bos, Brüll, Henny, *Maatschappijstructuren in beweging*, p. 25 (uitg. Vrij Geestesleven, Zeist, 1973)

Steiner developed Anthroposophy in the early part of the century. It was out of this wisdom of man that he also sought to give the impetus for a healing social impulse after the debacle of the First World War.* While the initiative to renew society through the creation of three distinct social spheres failed in 1919–21, other social endeavours have grown from the same impulse. One of these is the Netherlands Pedagogical Institute, or NPI International, which has sought to promote social and human development in modern organisational life during the last twenty years.

THE DEVELOPMENT AND WORK OF NPI

In the late 1940s and early 1950s Dr. Bernhard Lievegoed, a child psychiatrist with many years' experience in curative education, was asked by a number of Dutch industrialists whether he could help to solve the generational and labour-management conflicts which were appearing in their companies. He began to look into these questions by visiting organisations and acquainting himself with the ideas and methods of the newly emerging human-relations movement in the United States. In working on these problems Dr. Lievegoed also drew on his extensive knowledge of human development and on the work of Rudolf Steiner. His successful assistance to industry provided the impetus for Dutch industrialists and academicians to create a professorship in Social Pedagogy for him at the Economic University of Rotterdam. His request that a non-profit consulting and research institute be attached to the chair led to the creation of the Netherlands Pedagogical Institute in 1954.

From its inception the goal of NPI has been to foster social development within organisational life. This means that the

* For a description of the ideas underlying the threefold social movement see Rudolf Steiner, *The Threefold Social Order* (Anthroposophic Press, New York, 1970). Also Charles Waterman, *The Three Spheres of Society* (Faber and Faber, London, 1946)

staff has focused its attention more on areas such as communication, leadership, team building, personnel development, and organisational development than on improving the technical efficiency of work processes. In their work NPI staff members therefore seek to integrate the goal of economic efficiency with the human need of finding psychological and spiritual fulfilment in work.

In the last twenty years NPI has grown to include a full-time professional staff of twenty-eight. It has offices in Holland, France and South Africa and full-time representatives in Great Britain, Switzerland and Germany. The staff divides its time between research, consulting and training activities.

Consulting work has included a wide variety of projects in schools, hospitals, companies and governmental institutions. Typical projects include the following:

helping to develop new styles of management and leadership in companies;

developing strategies for change within automobile plants where labour turnover and absenteeism are high;

helping schools evolve new organisational forms more suited to educational needs and to the requirements of the teachers;

working with companies who have experienced a merger in order to find a new-company identity as well as new organisational forms;

improving individual motivation by helping organisations to communicate goals more clearly and to change their social climate through new forms of team-work;

training members of organisations in methods of training, communication, group work and organisational development;

working together with universities to develop new curricula and different forms of teaching.

A somewhat more unusual project was helping a religious order to understand why they were having difficulties finding new members and aiding them in finding new goals and new ways of working. Another involved working with dock workers in an area where strikes and crime were common-place. This long-term project involved finding forms of team-work which removed supervisors from their previously authoritarian roles, equalising the pay scale of the team and implementing job rotation.

Project work comes to NPI in the form of questions from individuals and organisations. If the request for assistance is judged to be genuinely motivated and the NPI members feel they can help, the project is usually taken on. This is also true for clients who have very limited funds at their disposal, as NPI has a sliding fee scale which can accommodate the less prosperous. As the Institute does not advertise, requests for assistance usually come from people who know something of its work and methods.

While a number of staff members may work on a large project, one person carries the main responsibility for it. Each senior member of NPI is in charge of two or more projects. However, in order to profit from the experiences of other staff members, projects are discussed regularly in the different working groups of the Institute.

In addition to project work NPI staff members conduct a variety of training courses, independently or within established training forums. Examples of this activity are the course(s) social skills and organisational development which NPI has offered in England with the Industrial Training Service (ITS). Areas in which NPI gives courses include management development, social skills, the design and implementation of learning situations, organisational change and development, communication and creative team-work. Courses last from one to three weeks and are intensive all-day experiences. Usually such courses consist of a mixture of introductory lectures, group work in which social questions are experienced and explored, along with concrete exercises and case studies. A given day in a social-skills workshop for managers might have the following content:

9.00–10.30	Lecture and dicussion on the phases of organisational development
10.30–11.00	Coffee
11.00–12.30	Groups discussion of a chosen problem area within a company (for example, motivation)
12.30–14.00	Lunch
14.00–15.30	Communication exercises plus evaluation and discussion
15.30–16.00	Tea or coffee
16.00–17.30	Prepared evaluation of the morning discussion (the purpose is then to look at problems of communication, leadership, problem solving etcetera, as they are experienced within the group)
17.30–18.00	Evaluation of the day

The goal of the research effort within NPI is to develop practical concepts and methods for social development which give individuals and organisations the possibility of seeing their situation clearly, of determining the direction in which they wish to move, and of beginning to take the first steps towards such a development.

NPI staff members develop new concepts from a combination of sources: the practical experiences of the staff, available literature in the field, and the relevant concepts and images from Anthroposophy. The research results are usually worked through by the whole staff and are then tested for their usefulness in field work. After a lengthy process of verification and modification these results are published. Unfortunately, most of this material is not available in

English. However, Professor Lievegoed's new book, *The Developing Organization*—now available in English—summarises a substantial portion of NPI's approach and research results.*

There are four main characteristics distinguishing NPI from other social development consulting and research groups: the internal organisation and method of working, the role of Anthroposophy, the conceptual models and tools which NPI employs, and the basic orientation which NPI staff bring to their work.

1. Process structure and group work: the internal organisation of NPI

One of NPI's main aims is to help organisations move from a relatively hierarchical and differentiated structure—which has a tendency to stifle individual creativity—towards a more flexible, less bureaucratic form in which the social needs of co-workers can be met. It has attempted to achieve the same aim internally. While the structure of the Institute initially had a form suited to the pioneering style of Professor Lievegoed, it has over the years moved towards a more differentiated flexible form in which the permanent staff members have fundamentally equal but rotating responsibilities. As will be seen later, this form is an effort to move towards the integrated clover leaf model of organisation which the NPI staff sees as a way of integrating the economic, technical and social sub-systems of modern organisations. NPI's present structure also attempts to take into account the different principles underlying social, economic and cultural life, as expressed in the threefold movement initiated by Rudolf Steiner.

If one looks at the organisation from the latter perspective one sees three main types of groups: study groups, social groups and work groups. The informal study groups can be seen as representing the cultural sphere in so far as they

---

* B. C. J. Lievegoed, *The Developing Organization* (Tavistock Publications, London, 1973)

provide a forum for individual initiative. The goal of the social groups is to determine the direction of the Institute's future development, and the conditions of its work based on the full equality of permanent staff members. The groups therefore represent the political or social sphere within NPI. In addition to the full-time professional staff assembly, other social groups include an elected rotating contact group which is responsible for facilitating social processes within the Institute and three project groups which respectively discuss goals and conditions for work in industry, education and government. These three project groups are also work groups which plan and carry out work in these three sectors. Large work groups include a project committee which co-ordinates the activities of the three groups, an elected administrative committee to handle the daily affairs of the Institute, and a Secretariat. Because of the internal and external services which these groups provide they are expressions of the economic sphere.

From the perspective of the previously mentioned clover leaf model the Institute has the following structure:

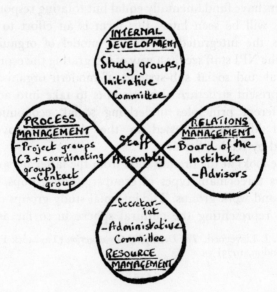

Here the different groups within NPI are seen in relation to the organisational processes which they seek to facilitate.*

The internal structure of the Institute is highly flexible and egalitarian as is indeed necessary for a group of rather individualistic professionals. Besides the unique organisational form of NPI, the staff's manner of working together should be mentioned. While multi-disciplinary team work is a popular slogan, especially in the academic world, it is seldom a reality. Although NPI still has some steps to take in order fully to utilise the diverse professional capabilities of its staff, they have moved towards realising this goal. The staff does meet as a whole every Saturday morning and genuine exchanges of information and insight do take place in these meetings as well as in the once-a-month internal work weeks. In addition the staff devotes four weeks a year to the discussion and development of new concepts and methods of social development. This activity offers the possibility for individual staff-members to gain new perspectives and to avoid the occupational hazard of intellectual stagnation.

2. Anthroposophy and social development

While NPI does not seek to propagate the ideas of Anthroposophy in its work, Anthroposophy does play an important role in the life of the Institute. This is because staff members find in Anthroposophy a path of knowledge essential for their work. In particular it provides a rich perspective of human evolution, basic concepts about man and the cosmos, and guidelines for a disciplined path of inner development. While it is not possible within this article to do justice to these aspects of Anthroposophy, a brief indication of their relevance to the activities of NPI can be given.

* For a description of the clover-leaf model see Lievegoed, *The Developing Organization*, pp. 80–9; also 'Turning a Pyramid into a Clover Leaf', *International Management*, August 1973)

The work of NPI is in social settings where poor communication, conflicts or limited social understanding has produced situations which people find intolerable and wish to change. These situations are becoming more commonplace at every social level. What explains these difficulties, or to put it more generally, what explains the growing asocial nature of our age? A variety of possible interpretations exists, from 'future-shock' and social psychosis to growing class consciousness. From the view of human evolution contained in Anthroposophy another perspective emerges, one which suggests that current forms of social crisis are related to the I-centred form of consciousness developed within Western culture during the last few hundred years.

If one examines ancient cultures or the less advanced cultures of today one finds a type of consciousness which still lives in the processes of nature and in the identity of family or clan. Laurens van der Post's description of the Bushmen of the Kalahari or Levi-Strauss's analysis of the primitive mind suggest a consciousness still capable of what Owen Barfield calls 'original participation' in the cosmos.* Rudolf Steiner described the development of human consciousness from this early form of original participation to our modern I-centred consciousness in considerable detail, pointing out that the development of modern science was inexorably linked to a type of consciousness which experienced itself as separated from its environment. Although he described this development in positive terms he also noted that the social consequences of our modern consciousness are destructive in so far as we experience our individual thoughts, feelings and needs and have difficulty in understanding the needs of others or the demands of a given social situation. He therefore portrayed the twentieth century as leading into a period of increasing social difficulty from which

* Owen Barfield, *Saving The Appearences: A Study of Idolatry* (Harcourt Brace and World, New York, 1965)

individuals and mankind as a whole would need to develop new social institutions and a new type of participative consciousness.*

This historical picture of human evolution provides the staff members of NPI with a certain framework for understanding present social conditions. It also suggests that such problems—whether they occur in business, schools or in the home—can be seen as providing essential opportunities for individual human development, for by confronting such difficulties the human ego is challenged to develop greater awareness. The staff members of NPI therefore tend to perceive social problems in terms of their potential for human growth, and they work to facilitate such growth by helping people to work out problems consciously.

The complex picture of human nature contained in Anthroposophy also plays an important role in the work of NPI. One small example is Rudolf Steiner's description of man as possessing the qualities of thinking, feeling and willing and his suggestion that we are conscious of our thoughts, dimly conscious of our feelings and largely unconscious of our will and how it works. This view provides a background for NPI's conception of training, group work and resistance to change. In training seminars NPI staff start with the more conscious conceptual element and then gradually seek to create opportunities in which the feelings and intentions of the participants can be consciously shared. NPI's concept of group development takes the same three elements into account by showing how a group moves from expected role behaviour in which ideas are primarily exchanged, through sets of crises, towards a mature creative group in which

---

* R. Steiner, *Die Soziale Grundforderungen unserer Zeit in geänderter Zeitlage* (Rudolf Steiner Nachlassverwaltung, Switzerland, 1963) and R. Steiner, *Wie kann die Seelische Not der Gegenwart überwunden werden?* (Rudolf Steiner Nachlassverwaltung, Switzerland, 1962)

group members share a common goal and have an understanding of each other's thoughts, feelings and intentions.

The question of resistance to change in individuals and groups is a difficult one. But here too NPI staff see the applicability of Rudolf Steiner's description. Resistance to a new idea at a conceptual level is the most overt and therefore the easiest to deal with. At the feeling level it becomes more problematical. Within organisations feelings of dislike or hatred, usually unconscious, are often created by changes where the individuals affected have not been involved in the planning. At the level of the will, deep fear can be called forth in an individual when, for example, his future in an organisation is threatened by a merger or by the addition of a younger and better educated colleague. At the level of feelings and will, resistance is difficult to deal with because it is seldom conscious. NPI regards time and assurances of security as necessary if these processes are to be made conscious and are to be overcome.

These examples suggest how one aspect of the anthroposophical image of man affects NPI's approach to problems of social development. Other examples will be mentioned in the discussion of NPI's conceptual models.

The relevance of the anthroposophical view of human evolution and of human nature to NPI's work has been indicated. The path of inner individual development described by Rudolf Steiner is at least of equal importance. As the literature on social change indicates, qualities of sensitivity, openness, empathy and genuineness are essential in a helping relationship, whether the goal of such change is individual therapy or organisational development.* Without these qualities a 'change agent' is unable to determine his client's real problems since a relationship of trust is usually

* See R. R. Carkhuff, *Helping and Human Relations*, Vol. I–II (Holt, Rinehart and Winston, New York, 1969) for a detailed discussion of the helping relationship.

essential before the real causes of a difficulty are articulated. Furthermore the change agent or therapist must manifest those qualities which he wishes to help others discover. Every person working in the social field is therefore sooner or later confronted with the question of how he can develop himself further in order to help others more effectively.

While there are many possible paths of self development, Anthroposophy provides both detailed guidelines for a slow process of inner growth and a description of the process which is occurring. An example of this approach are the six introductory exercises which Rudolf Steiner described as a way of achieving a healthy consciousness of oneself and of the world. These exercises are devoted to control of thought, control of action, control of feeling, positivity, openness and a sense of harmony in life.* They are aimed at strengthening and making conscious qualities which we all possess in varying degrees.

These exercises form a foundation in Anthroposophy for self development through meditation. The goal of such development is to become conscious as a spiritual as well as a physical being. While such a path of self development is not part of the official life of NPI, the nature of the work done and the goal of serving the needs of human development make it a freely chosen inner necessity for individuals. Without it the effectiveness of the work and the sense of unity within the Institute would be impaired.

3. Thinking in terms of development

In a consciously guided social change process, the fundamental concepts obviously play a vital role. They are needed to clarify the perception of the current situation, aid in the

---

* Ernst Katz in *Meditation: An Introduction* (Anthroposophical Society in America, 211 Madison Ave., N.Y.) provides a good introduction and description of these exercises. For a comprehensive treatment see Rudolf Steiner, *Knowledge of the Higher Worlds. How is it achieved?* (Rudolf Steiner Press, 1969)

diagnosis of problems and indicate the direction of change. Without conceptual models of some kind, social phenomena cannot readily be seen in relationship to one another, nor responded to adequately. Appropriate concepts are therefore the lenses which give at least partial vision to people concerned with social change.

Since social science literature is full of conceptual models of various kinds, the question arises as to which are most appropriate for understanding and guiding social processes. This was indeed a basic question for the members of NPI as they began their work in the early 1950s. They found considerable common ground with Kenneth Bouldings's classification of system complexity into nine levels that ranged from static framework systems through plant, animal, human and social systems to the transcendental level.* However, their review of social science literature led them to the conclusion that most existing concepts dealt with social systems as static, mechanistic or equilibrium oriented and not as living systems. They therefore searched for new models that were capable of describing and analysing social systems as these evolved in time.

NPI's initial focus in this search was the concept of development itself. In seeking to understand this process they were influenced by Goethe's scientific work, in particular his study of plants. Goethe's complex model of plant development contains the central principles of metamorphosis, increasing complexity and sacrifice or renunciation.† From these principles, Anthroposophy's emphasis on evolution, and practical experience, Prof. Lievegoed and his colleagues derived a general model of development. This can be related as follows: Development is a goal-directed

---

* Kenneth Boulding, 'General Systems Theory: The Skeleton of Science,' *Management Science*, vol. 2, no. 3, 1952

† Goethe, *Metamorphose der Pflanzen;* see E. Lehrs, *Man or Matter* (Faber and Faber, London 1958) for introduction to Goethean science

but discontinuous process which moves through a number of crises. It contains the following basic phases:

(a) growth of the whole system or large parts of it representing a quantitative increase;

(b) differentiation and specialisation so that functions previously carried out by the whole system can be concentrated in certain sub-systems;

(c) hierarchisation so that highly differentiated systems or functions can be governed by others, and

(d) integration, involving the formation of a new and more complex total entity.*

Based on this concept of development the staff of NPI has, in the past twenty years, evolved a variety of horizontal qualitative social development models which they believe are appropriate to the human and social sphere. These models have been worked out for individual, group, organisational and social development as well as for other areas such as learning, communication and social change strategy. The descriptive and general diagnostic capabilities of these models make them significant aids in understanding and guiding social change.

A description of NPI's model of organisational development and a method of organisational change called the U-Procedure follows.

The phases of organisational development

NPI initially evolved its model of organisational development for business concerns. These are defined as organisations working towards economic objectives that encompass an economic, technical and social sub-system.†

The model describes the evolution of such organisations from a pioneer phase, through a phase of differentiation or

* Lievegoed, *The Developing Organization*, p. 40
† Ibid, p. 45

183

scientific management towards a phase of integration. While the model is qualitative and longitudinal in nature in the sense that it describes development patterns over time—it also contains a number of vertical distinctions. Thus, besides distinguishing between the technical, economic and social sub-systems, NPI members visualise an organisation as a physical structure (that is, the plant and equipment), a process structure of work processes, a relational structure referring primarily to the quality and nature of human relationships, and an identity that is expressed in its concepts and goals. The first or pioneer phase of an organisation is seen as possessing the following basic characteristics:

The company was founded by an entrepreneur whose initiative lies in identifying an economic need and responding to it creatively.

Leadership in the pioneer organisation is clear—the pioneer is in charge and his authority is generally accepted because of his knowledge.

The economic sub-system is dominant in this first phase because the pioneer's main interest is economic performance—the satisfaction of his customers at a good profit. The technical and social sub-systems are not consciously developed because of limited specialisation and an informal, personal style of working.

The organisation has a shallow structure. There are generally no more than two levels of management.

The objectives of the company are clear and directly related to the quantity, quality and cost of the output.

Work motivation is generally high because the company usually has clear objectives and an informal style of working which gives individuals a chance to maximise their abilities and preferences.

The pioneer organisation's strength lies in its potential, its strong identity and its flexibility.

The weaknesses of this informal, family style organisation become readily apparent when the system is disturbed through external changes such as rapidly changing markets, new product technology or the need for large amounts of capital. Internally destabilising elements can be substantial increases in size, the need for specialising, or the retirement of the pioneer. Symptoms of a crisis in the pioneer organisations are often expressed in the following ways:

decreasing profits
increase of customer complaints
communication difficulties
decreasing manoeuvrability
declining motivation
leadership conflicts*

The crisis is obvious when workers question the pioneer's word.

When companies have successfully passed through the crisis of the pioneer phase they have in one way or another adopted the principles of scientific management. The implementation of these principles is seen by NPI staff as characterising the second major phase of organisation development. The main principles involved, are four:

1. Standardisation through which uniformity and interchangeability are introduced into work processes. Scientific planning and control over production is thus facilitated. An early example was standardisation in the production of the Model T Ford.
2. Mechanisation through which work and information processes are ordered and improved by replacing human labour by machines.
3. Specialisation as a correlate to the first two. Three forms of specialisation can be distinguished: functional

* Ibid, p. 57

185

specialisation, specialisation of management levels and specialisation of work processes. By the latter is meant the now common division of labour into planning, execution and control.

4. Co-ordination, in order to counteract the tendency towards fragmentation inherent in the implementation of the previous principles. Co-ordination efforts include unity of command, performance remuneration schemes and the like.*

Whereas NPI sees the economic sub-system as dominant in the first phase, the technical sub-system—the managing of people, things and processes—is seen as dominant during the second. The organisation becomes more hierarchical and specialised, requiring greater organisation to function effectively. One way of stating the difference between the pioneer organisation and the phase of scientific management is that the second phase is the antithesis of the first: 'rational instead of intuitive, mechanistic instead of organic, and impersonal instead of personal.'†

This change in structure and working style is essential for companies to grow to national and international proportions. However, over time this more rational system of organisation generates its own crisis. The problems associated with this crisis are well known to organisation development specialists. From NPI's point of view the main difficulties are these:

Rigidity: The loss of flexibility due to formalisation and becoming bureaucratic. Set procedures and structural forms are adopted which are difficult to change when new situations or needs arise.

Fragmentation: As the organisation becomes more specialised,

---

* Ibid, pp. 65–9

† NPI, *The Phases of Organizational Development* (unpublished stencil), p. 6

fiefdoms develop—some operating in a pioneer fashion—making communication and co-ordination very difficult. Company objectives are lost as each section or division sets its own goals. Often special co-ordinating committees are established but such steps are usually stop-gap measures.

Hierarchisation: Leadership becomes hierarchical and autocratic. The result is poor communication—the top not knowing what is happening, middle and lower levels not understanding what is wanted. Initiative at lower levels decreases. Staff-line problems of major proportions develop, focusing on authority. The distinction between line management and technical staff becomes artificial.

Motivation: As communication becomes more difficult, work more specialised, and the organisation more impersonal, individual motivation decreases. The individual experiences what Blauner refers to as meaningless, powerlessness, alienation and self estrangement.* Commitment to the company decreases, not only for workers but also for management.

When these symptoms appear the second phase has deteriorated and the organisation is no longer healthy.

The NPI staff then sees the necessity for the organisation to move in the direction of the integrated or clover leaf organisation. But whereas the movement from the pioneer stage to the second stage is felt to have a self-propelling character, movement towards the third stage is seen as involving conscious social development throughout the organisation.

Whereas in the first stage the economic sub-system was

* Robert Blauner, *Alienation and Freedom*, pp. 15–32 (University of Chicago Press, Chicago, Ill., 1964)

seen as dominant, and in the second the technical sub-system, the NPI staff considers the social sub-system to be of dominant importance in the integrated phase. This is because new styles of working together, and new styles of leadership need to be evolved so that co-workers can gradually meet their needs of self development in the working environment. Concretely this means an organisation where the hierarchical staff-line structure is supplanted by horizontal work processes in which working teams accept increasing responsibility for the planning, execution and control of work. This is only possible when the goals of the organisation are clear, and when management accepts and implements the ideas of self organisation and self control.

NPI's concept of the third stage is the clover leaf organisation previously described in relation to the Institute's internal structure. Within this concept four main functions are distinguished: information management, process management, resources management and relations management. The function of information managment is to assure the smooth functioning of the organization as a whole by providing relevant information. It is vital for policy-making, goal setting, motivating personnel and controlling resource use and work processes. Process management refers to production, information and decision-making processes. The management of resources includes both material and human resources—thus the personal function would fall into this area. Relations management is broadly defined to include relations with community groups, marketing and internal relations.

The clover leaf organisation is presented below, with the board of the company at the centre determining overall objectives and facilitating the functioning of the four processes:

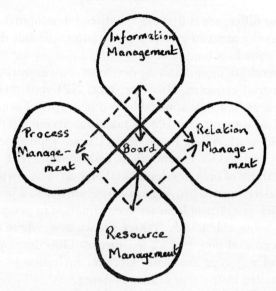

At the present time the clover leaf model is an effort to indicate the direction in which modern organisations might move. It is not a blueprint or model of structural change but an ideal model which seeks to stimulate thinking and helps organisations towards the management of their own developmental processes.*

Seen as a whole, NPI's model of organisational development is both an ideal-type description of the historical evolution of companies and a general picture of the individual biographies of organisations. The exception is the third or integration phase; most organisations are presently on the threshold of this phase, seeking organisational forms to avoid the shortcomings of the differentiated pyramid-structure.

If one looks at the phases of the model, the similarity to a biological process of growth can be seen, since the development is one from a flexible initial state through a process of differentiation to a state of higher integration. However,

* *International Management*, 'Turning a Pyramid into a Clover leaf'. Also Lievegoed, *The Developing Organization*, pp. 80–9

the major difference is that organisational development, like social development in general, is not automatic but dependent on conscious human action.

This model of organisational development was worked out for industrial concerns. However, most NPI staff members also see it as basically applicable to other types of organisations, if adjustment is made to take into account different goals and work styles. It has in fact been applied to professional and service organisations with success. NPI works with a variety of such developmental models. The purpose of such models is not to provide a concrete answer to a problem but rather to aid people to see their situation in perspective thereby being able to ask, 'Where are we now, where do we want to go and how can we get there?' Thus development models of this type are really more an invitation to dance than detailed instruction in how to dance.

The advantages of such models over quantitative causal models or equilibrium models or indeed of more conventional system models are many, as Robert Chin and others have noted.* Basically these advantages consist in the fact that such models supply a time perspective which facilitates analysis and goal directed action.

The U-Procedure

NPI staff members use development models in both course and project work. As some of these models are general in nature they are supported by a variety of more concrete methods aimed at helping people deal with particular organisational problems. One such method is the U-Procedure, a problem analysis and decision-making procedure.

In many organisations specific problems such as high absenteeism within a division, or continuing conflicts between

* Robert Chin, 'The Utility of System Models and Developmental Models for Practitioners', in Bennis, Benne and Chin, *The Planning of Change*, pp. 201–15 (Holt, Rinehart and Winston, New York, 1962)

the engineering and marketing staff keep occurring. Initially ad hoc efforts are made to solve these difficulties but as they keep occurring a more basic analysis and change seems called for. The U-Procedure is designed to facilitate this more basic analysis and change. It suggests a series of steps whereby the phenomena associated with the concrete problem are assembled, the system characteristics are analysed, and the basic concepts and goals of the organisation, division or department are brought to consciousness. This then leads to a point where a discussion of basic goals and ways of working can take place.

In such a discussion the members of an organisation are consciously confronted with the goals and concepts of their organisation. From this confrontation new goals and principles for work can be chosen, plans made and concrete changes implemented.

The U-Procedure consists of seven basic steps which can be summarised as follows:

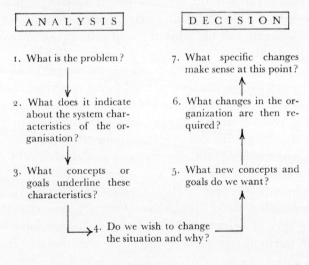

Past oriented   Present   Future oriented

This procedure takes a number of days to work through adequately with a group of managers or workers, or both. Its seeming simplicity is deceptive.

The first three steps are past oriented and basically conceptual in nature in the sense that a problem is being analysed.

In step four the participants are in the present and must decide whether they wish to commit themselves to change. The last three steps are then future directed and are devoted to gradually making concrete the proposals for change. Whereas the first three steps are conceptual and the last three connected to the will of the participants, the middle step requires a strong feeling of enthusiasm and commitment in order to awake the will of the participants to work out and implement concrete change proposals.

Another aspect of the procedure is that it moves from the concrete physical dimension of a work process, for example, to the concepts which underlie that process, to the basic goals and identity of the organisation in which that process occurs. It therefore helps in making conscious what Berger and Luckmann call the 'objective and subjective dimension' of social reality.*

The process is then reversed and the movement in steps 5, 6 and 7 is from the conceptual level to the concrete. Seen as a whole the U-Procedure is an aid in consciously understanding and restructuring the organisational environment. This method, along with other methods like it, augments and helps make concrete the development models that NPI uses in its work.

Anthroposophy provides a variety of perspectives for understanding the U-Procedure. Basically one could say it is a way of helping individuals to experience something of the spiritual essence or being of an organisation. It can

* P. Berger and T. Luckmann, *The Social Construction of Reality*, A Treatise in the Sociology of Knowledge, (Doubleday, 1966)

be seen as facilitating such an experience by fostering a kind of Imagination through a full and lively description of phenomena, an element of Inspiration through the effort of seeing the basic characteristics of the whole organisation and an Intuition of the essence of the organisation through having understood the concepts and goals on which the organisation is based. From another point of view, the U-Procedure can be seen as a way of understanding the being of the organisation by gradually bringing to consciousness and removing the physical, etheric and astral layers of organisational life.

However it is viewed, it is important to note that this procedure often helps individuals to have a deep experience of the organisation they work in. When this is the case, great inner tension can result as a person is faced with a choice of either consciously connecting himself with the future development of the organisation or leaving it because it does not conform to his own values.

NPI's model of organisational development and the U-Procedure have been described in order to indicate the nature of the Institute's conceptual tools. These tools are not only unique in themselves, but they offer a way of working with social and organisational questions that do not lead to prescribed answers. Rather they lead to an increased social awareness and social choice for the individuals involved. In this sense they are tools that enlarge the area of human awareness and freedom.

4. Personal growth and social development

Three distinguishing characteristics of NPI have been indicated: the internal structure and method of working, the role of Anthroposophy, and the nature of the conceptual tools used. A fourth element can be added, NPI's basic orientation towards social and organisational problems.

NPI staff feel there are no uniform or general solutions to social and organisational questions. While general patterns can be seen in group or organisational development, the particular organisation or group always possesses a unique identity. NPI members therefore try to help people evolve individual ways of dealing with their particular situations. The successful committee system in one school is thus not automatically suggested as the answer for another, despite the occasional temptation to do so.

Another aspect of NPI's approach is that staff members do not seek to provide answers to problems as such. Rather they attempt to work as speaking partners and stimulators who provide concepts and training in social skills and techniques which aid people in analysing their situation and altering it in a desired direction.

There are two main reasons why NPI is not a problem solving Institute, one negative, the other positive. The negative one is that solutions from outside are seldom accepted or implemented, as peace-makers on the individual and international scale have experienced. The positive one is that people develop themselves in consciously coming to grips with their organisational problems. Because NPI staff members perceive social difficulties as a developmental opportunity for people, their approach and methods are aimed at stimulating social insight and personal growth. A third characteristic of NPI's orientation is connected with the idea of development. Many current social problems stem from the fact that people either wish to preserve existing habits and customs, thereby contributing to social stagnation, or wish to see their social ideals realised immediately, a viewpoint which tends towards social chaos. Since the founding of NPI, Professor Lievegoed and his colleagues have sought to stimulate a middle path of consciously guided social change which avoids both extremes.

THE FUTURE DIRECTION OF NPI

The further development of NPI is difficult to foresee as it is dependent on the kinds of questions which the Institute receives. Until recently most requests for assistance have come from organisations. Yet some recent questions and the general state of society suggests that future work might develop in two additional directions. One is more in the macro-social area, dealing with such issues as relations between consumers and producers, the state's role in education and large-scale social planning for urban areas. The other direction is that of aiding young people and adults in coping with modern life as individuals, more the educational and therapeutic area. Some NPI members are already heavily involved in developing a Free University out of the many insights provided by Rudolf Steiner. Others are working with crisis centres, retirement homes and state organised youth training programmes. The picture is therefore one of increasing diversification in activities.

At the same time NPI is experiencing a process of internationalisation. Groups directly associated with NPI are working in France, Germany, England, Switzerland, South Africa and Brazil.

How these new initiatives will develop and how they will affect the Institute in Zeist is still uncertain. But it seems likely that NPI will increasingly evolve towards an international network of groups which seek to promote practical social understanding at a time when such understanding is vitally needed.

(This article is dedicated to the members of NPI for the time and effort they have spent in trying to initiate me into the intricacies of social change processes.)

FURTHER READING

Rudolf Steiner, *World Economy* (Rudolf Steiner Press, London, 1972)

B. C. J. Lievegoed, *The Developing Organisation* (Tavistock Publications Ltd., 1973)

Folkert Wilken, *The Liberation of Work. The elimination of strikes through associative organisation of enterprise* (Routledge and Kegan Paul, 1969)

9. RELIGIOUS RENEWAL

The work of the Christian Community

by OLIVER MATHEWS

Religion is concerned primarily with people. It is people who make the society in which they live. If that society is unsatisfactory, it is only people who can alter it.

Certain almost unconscious assumptions have permeated society today, namely that the paramount influences at work on this earth are heredity and environment. What religion has said and done in the past is regarded more and more as irrelevant. What kind of a religious approach would be experienced as significant today?

Is birth simply the arrival of a new human body to be registered and included in a computerised census? Is marriage nothing more than a legalised contract which can be legally annulled? Is death mainly a question of striking a name off a register and disposing of the body in a way as dignified as possible?

Many people go through inner crises today. Some of these end in suicide or a mental breakdown. Some work through to an inner conviction that they are not just the product of heredity and environment and, much as they may owe to their heredity and ancestry, they are something in themselves and are ready and capable to begin shaping their own lives, and to share in the shaping of society. Has a living religion something to contribute to this?

In 1921, a group of people who were mostly in their early twenties, but including Dr. Friedrich Rittelmeyer—one of the foremost leaders of the Lutheran church in Germany—had come to believe that profound help for a renewal of religious life could arise out of what they had discovered in Rudolf Steiner's Anthroposophy. They therefore approached Dr. Steiner and asked for his advice and guidance. He agreed to meet them. They put many questions. His main reply was that if the religious life was to be renewed today it would only be through a renewal of the sacraments.

This was the first of several meetings with Rudolf Steiner of a growing number of individuals interested in religious questions and culminated in the decision of forty-five men and women to found, with Dr. Steiner's help and direction, a movement for religious renewal.

The foundation of the Christian Community

The whole of this volume is concerned with activities which owe their origins to the teaching of Rudolf Steiner. In describing the Christian Community's work for religious renewal, one is faced with a paradox. The movement could not have been born without Rudolf Steiner. Yet he did not found it, and it exists alongside the Anthroposophical Society and the various branches of its activities as a separate movement. The Christian Community exists for the renewal of the religious life, through the renewal of the sacraments. This is not quite the same as drawing one's vision and impulse from the spiritual world and enabling it to flow into the various branches of culture or into the practical work of the world through one's own striving. The sacraments are given complete. The priest who administers the sacraments in their new form has no power to alter them; indeed he makes a vow that he will alter nothing on his own initiative.

Something more needs to be said about the paradox already mentioned. When the Christian Community was founded Rudolf Steiner spoke repeatedly and with great emphasis on the significance of the renewal of the sacraments. What he said was spoken specifically to the priests in relation to their special task. It is necessary that more of what he said should be passed on in order to clear up any difficulties that could arise as to the relationship of the two movements. One difficulty has been that until one has absorbed what has been said, has put it into practice and it has begun to form part of one's experience, one is not in a position to convey adequately what is involved.

Rudolf Steiner continually asserted that the time has come when it is necessary for humanity to grow beyond a simple acceptance of Christianity and to penetrate ever more deeply in consciousness to the understanding of the Mystery of Golgatha; but, at the same time, he continually emphasised that this event was a Mystery, the full significance of which would only be realised at the end of earth evolution.

The centre of this evolution is Christ Jesus himself, and what He did and continues to do. The sacraments, from the beginning, Steiner said, are a continuation of Christ's deed. What Christ, as a culmination of his incarnation requested the disciples to do, namely to assimilate his body and his blood, which He was now identifying with the elements of the earth, He continued to elaborate with his disciples during the days between the Resurrection and the Ascension, when Christ withdrew, not from the earth, but into the life sphere of the earth. Henceforth He could unite with the elements anywhere, in so far as human beings gave him the opportunity of doing so.

There is no need at this point to trace the gradual disappearance of the experience of the transubstantiation, the gradual clouding of the instinctive connection with spiritual realities which survived in some measure until a century or so ago. The immediate point that Rudolf Steiner made clear was that the original author and the main actor in the sacraments is Christ himself. They are a continuance of his deed.

There is a difference between demonstrating in detail what has to be done in order that something may happen and explaining why it has to happen. All that Steiner said to the founders of the Christian Community is sheer Anthroposophy applied to a particular task; but the actual foundation, which took place in the Goetheanum in September 1922, was an event, the fruits of which have been experienced ever since in the celebration of the sacraments.

What Rudolf Steiner gave as Anthroposophy not only throws light on every aspect of human knowledge, but can lead to effective action in every task of modern life— including that of the priesthood. What the priest is called upon to do in his sphere stands alongside the activities of doctors, farmers, teachers, artists, social reformers, scientific investigators. Each works as a disciple among disciples, giving his service to his fellow men, among any of whom also the aspiration can arise to become a disciple himself. At the centre of the priest's work lies the caring for the sacraments, and so we must look at this work in a little more detail.

Ordination and priesthood

The sacraments, as Rudolf Steiner showed, are deeds to be enacted to establish a communion between the spiritual world, mankind and the earth. When a ritual is celebrated something happens. Once placed in human hands it is possible for them to be misused with devastating effect. The greatest evil is often derived from corruption of the greatest good. Wherever and whenever rituals have been celebrated, there has always been a form of ordination. There is need of a priesthood and a lifelong vow that the sacraments may be protected.

In the ceremony of ordination, which is woven into the

Communion service of the Christian Community, the candidate receives the emblems of his office, is annointed with consecrated oil, and is introduced stage by stage into the celebration of the sacrament.

In past epochs the training of a priest was a path of initiation. A human being became a priest because he was an initiate. The ultimate authority and guidance in every sphere—healing, teaching, the ordering of social life, the direction of agriculture etcetera—was ultimately under the direction of an initiate, who was also a priest. Today, for the most part, clergymen, doctors, teachers, politicians, farmers are not initiates. A beginning has to be made, and is being made through Anthroposophy, in order that spiritual knowledge shall flow into all activities. So it is that a priest, just because he can lay no claim to initiation, needs to receive the power and authority to enable him to become the mediator of sacramental acts.

The ordination itself contains an implication and a warning. Having been trained and ordained, the priest now takes his further evolution largely into his own hands. He makes a vow before he is ordained not to alter the sacraments on his own initiative, and to abide by the regulations governing the priestly activities. He is granted full freedom of teaching. He acknowledges the obligation for mutual support between priests and their families. He accepts the judgement of the hierarchy (referred to later) on his priestly conduct. The priesthood is open to women.

Traditionally, the task of the priest is threefold: sacramental, prophetic and pastoral. The sacramental task, apart from the words and gestures of the rituals, includes everything that has to do with vestments, altar, chapel, the elements involved in sacramental acts, the vessels and accoutrements. General directions for all this were given by Rudolf Steiner. The detailed fulfilment lies with the priest, in collaboration with artists, architects, craftsmen, and the members of his congregation. The final word in all these matters lies with the priest.

The prophetic task includes everything that has to do with teaching and instruction. The priest has complete freedom in this realm, provided of course that his teaching does not undermine the sacramental task he has been ordained to fulfil. The theology and psychology of the Christian Community is drawn from Anthroposophy. This means that the priest has a new light to throw on the Bible, on Church history and world history, on nature, literature, social and economic problems, and in particular on the ideals, failures, sufferings and anxieties which human beings meet in their daily life, in other words in their destinies. Instead of imparting dogmas or doctrines which his congregations are supposed to accept, he has to draw for his teaching on the nature of the universe in so far as he understands it. He has to be awake continually to the actual needs of the people before him. He has also to recognise that no one is under any obligation to accept what he says. The truths he imparts need to be self-evident.

The pastoral task is the care of souls. More will be said of this later. The main emphasis is the recognition of the eternal value of every individual spirit, each involved in a unique destiny, and the acknowledgement that Christ is the higher self of humanity, the mediator of the higher self of every individual, and leads always through freedom.

To put it in an exaggerated picture, it is conceivable that a congregation could consist mainly of people whom the conventional world considered criminals, many of whom might be more outstanding personalities than the priest, but who recognised the presence and power of Christ in the sacramental acts which the priest was empowered to celebrate and the truth of the teaching he was enabled to impart.

Congregations in fact are extraordinarily varied, largely because they are not collections of people who are emotionally or intellectually agreed on a particular attitude of life or conduct, but are individuals of very different backgrounds seeking to work out their destinies in a time when human destiny is in confusion. The work of religious renewal is concerned with the forming of free communities, in which the community arises out of the free will of the individuals who compose it, communities in whom a new sense of discrimination, concern for humanity, and personal dedication may arise and flow into the tasks and activities of private and public life.

The renewal of the sacraments

Since the heart of the work of the Christian Community lies in the renewal of the seven sacraments, it is necessary to say something about each of these, besides other aspects of the work which are related to this central task.

This description has already begun in what has been said about ordination. The ordination is not a ceremony which any seeker would be likely to experience to begin with, but it has been mentioned first, because the work of the Christian Community could not begin (although preliminary work had been done), until there were ordained priests able to celebrate the sacraments. The ordination of the forty-five founders of the movement took place in the presence and under the guidance of Rudolf Steiner at Dornach in the autumn of 1922.

The other sacraments will now be described in turn. The distinction between a religious life related to the sacraments and other forms of cultural life is that it is to begin with based mainly on *observation* of ceremonies (in which all the senses are involved), and in the accompanying inner *experiences*. Instruction does not play a central part at the beginning. The nearest parallel is drama. The central act of the Christian Community, the Communion service, known as the Act of Consecration of Man, is a drama with invisible participants, who are addressed in the ceremony. The celebrating priest is the mouthpiece both of the spiritual world—for the words he speaks are not his words, nor do his gestures and movements derive from his own personality —and of the human beings who, in the full sense of the word, are behind him.

Religious forms, until recently, have had the task of keeping the doors open for religious experience in a humanity which was descending ever more deeply into incarnation. For a large number of people in the modern world, the doors of the spiritual world are now closed, so deeply closed that, for many, it is a question today whether there was ever anything behind those doors. This cutting-off was a necessary process. When the prodigal has spent all, the wealth of tradition has come to an end, the outer world has become husks, he finds 'himself', and through this discovery can set off on his journey to the Father. The experience of the self emerges so to speak in exile.

According to Rudolf Steiner sacraments are always related to the stage human consciousness has reached. The rituals which he was able to bring from the spiritual world stimulate the awakening self, the true individuality.

The new forms of worship provide a foundation for a new approach to prayer. It becomes more and more a question whether human beings can live balanced lives in the modern world without the practice of prayer and meditation.

Night by night we take into our sleep and into our subconscious or unconscious what we have poured, or allowed to be poured, into our conscious mind during the day. We emerge next day one night richer in virtue or in villainy, a matter of no little concern to the social life. To what extent is each individual building or undermining society? We become increasingly aware today that we are walking on ground beneath which simmer subterranean fires.

The experience of the sacraments awakens the realisation that there is a power at work in the universe, healing and sustaining, which is more powerful than the powers of darkness and destruction. This opens the way to the possibility of private prayer. Two of the most widely read publications of the Christian Community are Friedrich Rittelmeyer's *Meditation* and Adam Bittleston's little book, *Meditative Prayers for Today*, both written as an aid to the practice of private prayer. The habit of praying has died away in this century, in which the prevailing views have no room for God, or any clear concept of a being capable of prayer. People seek to know how prayer may lead to guidance and strength for one's personal life, and how to direct one's prayers for the living and the dead.

The altar and the chapel

The altar is the indispensable centre of sacramental worship. It is at the same time the image of a tomb and a table. It announces that every time one comes to worship one approaches the threshold which one crosses when one dies, and implies that a communication with the world beyond it can take place during life. It is a table because one partakes of a meal, the main substance of which is imparted just at this threshold where heaven and earth meet.

All through the centuries it was the altar which built the churches. The altar must be there, and, in a pioneer stage, may be a table or a chest in a private room adapted for the occasion. The church is built, or a room is shaped and decorated, to provide a worthy environment and protection for the holy act, and is inevitably an expression of what emerges from that act. Whenever one enters the chapels of the Christian Community one will experience something of the atmosphere created by the sacraments, which by no means implies uniformity.

Baptism and Confirmation

Baptism is celebrated as soon after birth as possible, though children who have not been baptised may at their request be baptised before Confirmation. Baptism is primarily an aid to incarnation. What happens in the neighbourhood of a little child, whose soul is completely open, works deeply into the whole constitution of the child and can have a life-long effect.

Through the sacrament the child is, as it were, touched and blessed by Christ as it descends from the realm of light into the realm of darkness. The child hears its name, which is to indicate its identity, spoken repeatedly in the sacrament. The godparents, as representatives of the human community, (who need not be members of the movement) are reminded that they have undertaken in freedom a responsibility of destiny. The body of the child is blessed with water, salt and ash, which have been consecrated in the course of the ceremony. The earthly temple in which the soul is to dwell during its earthly life is consecrated with representatives of the earth.

As Baptism is mainly confined to infants, so Confirmation is celebrated for the adolescent, usually from the age of fourteen. Adults are not confirmed. Neither Baptism nor Confirmation are a condition for taking part in services or other activities, nor are children who are baptised or confirmed claimed as members. These sacraments are blessings bestowed by the spiritual world at particular stages of incarnation.

A children's service and religious teaching are available for all children from the age of six. Children's holidays are arranged for any children who care to take part, usually in a country district with planned daily activities, games, walks, getting up to see the sunrise, helping with the chores and the cooking. On one holiday the children baked their own bread, and helped to build a kiln to bake the pottery they had made.

Preparation classes for Confirmation are held from the age of thirteen. The Gospel and the sacraments are taught as guides and pathways which enable each person to follow the path of his own individual destiny in freedom and in common with his fellowmen. The ceremony of Confirmation is celebrated in conjunction with the Communion service, and the children receive the sacrament for the first time. The day is arranged as a festival and is experienced by most children as an event in their lives.

Holiday camps are arranged for teenagers, which are also open to young people not connected with the movement. Youth conferences are arranged where possible.

Marriage

The relationship of man and woman has entered a new phase in this century, which can hardly be assessed by the study of physiology and psychology. The emancipation of women, which has taken place in this century, is something new in human history. Women are awakening to a consciousness of their individual egos, and are asserting what up to now has been the prerogative of the man. Basically this is an emancipation of spirits, not an emancipation of bodies as it tends to be regarded. This has far-reaching social implications with regard to home, work and children. It is more difficult to be a woman today in what is a man-made civilisation. The future of society depends more on the women than on the men. Is woman to assert her new-found maleness or draw on her womanliness and with her new-found initiative steer society towards a more human pattern? A religious movement which is aware of the situation, and has a Sacrament of Marriage which is a confirmation of the constructive side of this new development, has a contribution to make to this aspect of the social problem.

The marriage ceremony of the Christian Community emphasises the relationship of two independent spirits who in freedom resolve to enter into community of life and seek the witness and the blessing of Christ on their resolve. The ceremony includes the presence of two witnesses, who know the man and woman and support their decision. Solemn words are spoken to the witnesses, reminding them that they have heard the public avowal of this man and woman, and calling upon them to give living aid to this resolve. It is emphasized that a religious ceremony is an act fulfilled in freedom. It contains no legal formula. The registry office form, which gives the marriage a legal basis, needs to be completed independently of the marriage sacrament.

Counselling

Not many people today are concerned with sin, but how many people are free from worry or anxiety? Mental illness, to a great extent caused by the increasing tensions of modern life, or the sheer boredom and purposelessness of existence, is filling the mental hospitals and is the cause of widespread absenteeism.

Humanity as such has passed through a stage of childhood and adolescence, accompanied by stages of authority and law, with which religion had much to do. Today humanity is striving, though for the most part subconsciously, towards adulthood. We feel constrained by rules and regulations. We have yet to learn that, independent of all legality, we live in a world in which we ourselves are causes, and that we reap the result of our own actions. Growing beyond the stage of legality, we can become aware of quite other causes and effects. We experience the working of destiny. We are all actors in the unfolding of a drama. The situations in which we find ourselves are the result of previous actions. Moreover, what happens in the next act will depend on how we are dealing with the present situation.

Confession and absolution have no meaning in this context. In the Christian Community we have the sacrament of

'Sacramental Consultation'. A priest is always available for a conversation on any subject. He is not there to exercise any authority, nor primarily even to advise, but as a sympathetic listener. If a conversation becomes sufficiently serious, both may feel that something more than a human exchange is called for. The priest puts on his vestments to mark that henceforth the spiritual world is invited to take part. Both parties are seeking the light which Christ can throw on a situation. At the end, the short words of the ritual are spoken which concern suffering and grace, love and peace, a help and stimulus to find one's own way and shoulder one's own destiny.

Death and survival

The rituals still to be mentioned are those which are related to the passing of the soul into the spiritual world at death. Children are not fully incarnated. They have yet to fulfil an earthly destiny. A different form of burial is celebrated for a child which has not yet reached puberty. It is a ceremony which breathes an atmosphere of grief. It is a matter of deep sorrow when a soul has to withdraw before coming fully to the earth.

The indulgence in grief at the passing of an adult, which is understandable and in a measure unavoidable, can be in part selfish. The burial services for an adult leave little room for grief. They are entirely positive. They proclaim the entry of the soul into a new kind of activity. Those present are enjoined to raise their thoughts to the realm where the departed is already finding his way. Words which convey the powerful and positive promises of Christ concerning the transformation of death form part of the ceremony. The purport of the ceremony is not to say farewell to a being passing into a distant and unattainable country, but rather to establish a new relationship which need never be severed.

The seventh sacrament, 'The Last Anointing', which is

celebrated for someone on the point of death, one could describe as an aid to dying, a help to pass the threshold as consciously as possible and with the assurance that Christ leads souls from existence to existence. This sacrament can be celebrated if the person is already unconscious. It can, and sometimes does, lead to recovery.

A memorial service is held for the departed on the first Saturday possible after the burial. The memorial service takes the form of a celebration of the Act of Consecration of Man. Black vestments are worn. The Gospel reading is the resurrection Gospel of Easter Sunday. A special prayer for the one who has died is spoken at the end. The Communion service assumes that the dead can share in our worship.

It may not be immediately apparent what relationship burial services can have on the social life. Long before the Christian Community was born, Rudolf Steiner made the statement that the right kind of burial services were more important for the social life than many resolutions carried in committees. People seldom die with their life work completed. They are still concerned that the tasks they have initiated shall be carried to completion by those who remain behind. How can they communicate? Only if a new relationship is established between the living and the dead. This the burial service can initiate, and the Communion service continue.

Festivals

Festivals are celebrated in the Christian Community not only as a reminder of the events at the beginning of our era, but to bring to experience the earthly and cosmic re-enaction of these events year by year. The festivals reveal how Christ partakes in the rhythms of the earth and the heavenly bodies and can be experienced differently in the different seasons. We learn to know more about Christ in his fullness in so far as we are able to relate ourselves sensitively to the modes of the festivals as revealed in the 'Epistles' which provide a changing framework to the central ritual, and the progress of the Biblical readings throughout the year. Together these emphasise and illuminate the metamorphoses of nature and the metamorphoses of human consciousness in the different seasons.

The Bible

There is no book which has had such a universal impact as the Bible. It is translated into nearly a thousand languages. In some of the countries behind the iron curtain there are people ready to risk their lives for a portion of the Bible. There is something in the human soul which, in spite of distorted political, economic or scientific teaching, responds to what is virtually a textbook of the human self. From a mythical background describing the creation of the world and of mankind, and the ensuing separation of man from his divine origin, which set him on the path of his earthly destiny, there emerges a story of a people whose God means 'I am'. This people evolves a form which is a kind of microcosm, reflecting with its twelve tribes an image of the macrocosm, a race constantly struggling with its imperfections and the resulting crises, yet conscious of a divine mission.

Out of this people is born eventually Jesus who became the Christ, in whom was manifested a divine 'I am' which is to become the indwelling core of the human being, himself a microcosm, on an individual scale.

The Old Testament describes the separation from the spirit, and the descent into earthly incarnation, which is repeated in the conception, birth and development of every child. The New Testament describes the path blazed by Christ Jesus, which if followed to the end leads to the transformation of man and of the earth. The Bible contains three layers, the historical, the moral and the spiritual. The moral element is that which has been mainly emphasised in Protestantism. In this century, influenced by the growing expertise in historical, archaeological and documentary research, an attempt has been made, not without some success, in relation to the Old Testament, to establish the historical accuracy of the Bible. The deeper spiritual layer cannot be revealed by these methods. The events which describe the nexus of divine and human, related in the New Testament, cannot be outwardly proved. They are matters on which every individual has to make up his own mind.

Before the time of Protestantism, the Bible was not in the hands of the laity, and to the priest who sought to deepen his inner life it was an esoteric book. We have now come to the time when there can no longer be a sharp distinction between the disciple and the multitude. The deeper spiritual layer needs to be made public. This has been made possible by the teachings of spiritual science, which centre on what Rudolf Steiner continually refers to as 'The Mystery of Golgotha'.

The celebration of sacraments, which is the central role of the priest, is inevitably accompanied by the teaching role in which the study and exposition of the Bible plays a central part. To teach adequately, a priest has to know something of two other books: first, the 'book of the earth' as discovered by the sciences of today, and supplemented by the teachings of spiritual science. Religion can no longer flourish as something isolated and separated from every other knowledge. Secondly, he needs to know something of the book of the human soul, a psychology of the inner life. In all this he is beholden to Anthroposophy. Now that Anthroposophy has bridged the gap between religion and science, theology can no longer be the exclusive domain of the clergy. It will remain a central theme of their study and teaching, but they will be open to what can come from any source, including members of their congregations.

Healing

In the Christian Community there is no special practice of spiritual healing, though nothing would be put in the way of its taking place. Those who are responsible for the Christian Community are persistent advocates of anthroposophical medicine, biodynamic agriculture, the healing qualities of Steiner's educational methods, and the practice of the arts.

Nevertheless the celebration of sacraments is a long term healing process, for the individual, for the community, and for the earth. The sacraments awaken a response in the whole human being, establishing harmony and balance. Many physical ailments have a psychological origin. The sacraments act as a kind of prophylactic against disease. What radiates from the sacramental act at the soul level can resolve disharmonies and tensions without the need to lift them into consciousness. Rudolf Steiner gave a course for doctors and priests indicating how the practice of medicine and the celebration of the sacraments can supplement one another.

Social work

Anyone working for religious renewal is almost inevitably involved in some kind of social work. In larger congregations on the Continent congregational helpers and nurses are, so to speak, on the staff. The villages of the Camphill movement endeavour, where possible, to find a place for a priest and chapel in their village communities. Yet it would be true to say both of the Anthroposophical Movement and the Christian Community, that, called as we are to deal with the effects of modern civilisation, the main aim is to shape a society in which a good deal of what has to be dealt with by the social services becomes less necessary.

Relationship to other religions

The simplest comment on the relationship of the Christian

Community to other Christian Churches is found in one of the sentences of the Creed, which is spoken not as a confession of faith, but rather as a statement of certain fundamental facts which we acknowledge. One sentence proclaims that members of a community which is aware of the Christ within may feel themselves united in a church to which all belong who are aware of Christ's health-bringing power. In other words there is an invisible universal Church manifested wherever Christ is actually at work.

No one who joins the Christian Community is required to leave any other movement. Members of the Christian Community are at liberty to associate and join in the activities of any other movement. The religious life of mankind whenever it is alive, is a matter for respect and interest, not something to be contraverted.

The congregations

A congregation in the Christian Community can only be a group of free individuals, who find in the sacraments an experience which stimulates the inner life, particularly that element which leads to individual judgement and responsibility.

Such a group of free individuals can have no illusion of present perfectibility or a sense of superiority over their fellow men. It is rather a group who, aware of their own shortcomings and the shortcomings of others, seek to understand rather than to criticise, a group which is convinced that the spiritual world is not only pointing to some far off perfection but can work through all human beings today, as they are.

The altar and the sacraments provide a focal point from which light, warmth and power can radiate into the world. What radiates from the sacrament can be carried into home and work as a kind of leven which works by no rules.

214

Membership

Sacraments, study groups, conferences and literature are available for everyone. One does not have to become a member to partake in the life of the movement. Only adults who have had ample time for their own experience of the movement, and to whom all information has been made available, are admitted as members.

Behind every movement is a spiritual being, who has no earthly body, but, to manifest on earth, needs an earthly vehicle. The sacraments are, so to speak, presided over by such a being. Members constitute the cells of an earthly body through which the being of the community can work. Therefore to become a member is to enter into a spiritual commitment, which involves no prescribed outer obligations, though it is largely members who fulfill the practical work of the community.

The organism of the Christian Community

The movement is constituted as an organism rather than an organisation. Though there is necessarily a hierarchy as a protection for the sacraments, it is not a pyramidal structure, rather centrifugal and centripetal, a radiation from the centre to the periphery and back. At the centre is the 'Archleader', the *Erzoberlenker*, who with two *Oberlenkers* ('over-leaders') constitute a kind of triumvirate. Alongside them are four Lenkers, a name which we have now adopted internationally, as it implies guides and steerers rather than bishops. These constitute a circle of seven in whose hands are the main decisions. There are also other Lenkers who have territorial responsibilities.

The point is not that one gives orders and the other obeys. Surrounding the Lenkers are the circles of priests in the various countries or regions. The priests who are working in their congregations are in touch with the Lenker, as the Lenker is in touch with the centre of the movement. Synods of priests are held locally, and international synods in most years, so that the centre knows what the periphery is thinking, and the endeavour is made that every main decision has the backing of the whole priesthood. The priest is surrounded by his congregation, the members of which have each a variety of connections with the outer world. All this presents a picture of living organism which can be indefinitely extended.

Every priest has complete freedom in the way he does his work. The members co-operate out of free choice, and are bound by no doctrine. The priest has no authority over the members of his congregation, who are under no obligation to recognise the hierarchy. The hierarchy provides a recognisable order and mutual discipline for the priesthood.

Last, but most important, the sacraments are celebrated to make possible an immediate experience of the supersensible world. As for each person this communication is direct, the whole organism wherever it spreads, provides the opportunity for an ever increasing number of individuals to find a fulfilment of their own spiritual needs.

The movement which was founded in central Europe in 1922 has spread through many of the countries of Europe and reached Britain in 1929. It has since spread to America, Canada and South Africa. There are congregations in Brazil and Argentine. The sacraments are celebrated in the language of the country in which they are established.

The Anthroposophical Society and the Christian Community

From what has already been said it will be clear why the task of religious renewal had to be fulfilled in a separate movement. Nevertheless, in order to clear away possible misunderstandings, some further points need to be made. This is not easy as it is impossible to define a reality which is in constant metamorphosis. I feel however that it should be attempted by one who has lived with Anthroposophy since 1928 and with the Christian Community since 1929.

As human beings we are endowed with the faculties of thinking, feeling and willing. In ordinary human life they are never entirely separated. Behind every thought there is an element of feeling and willing. Nevertheless it is characteristic of today that there is a kind of short-circuiting of thinking and willing. The heart element seems to disappear. The fine accurate investigations of natural science inspire a powerful practical technology. A powerful will underlies the nihilistic thinking of today, which is not the will of the individual human spirit. Yet thinking is the instrument of human freedom, and is the faculty through which one consciously grasps the nature of the world and oneself.

In his lectures on Anthroposophy and Psychoanalysis Rudolf Steiner said that most people today are psychologically sick. In past centuries the religious conceptions of the world which people instinctively accepted as true, warmed the feelings and inspired the will. Today a material abstract view of the world, pervading education and underlying much of what is written or said, has become an unconscious assumption which is hardly ever challenged. There is nothing in it which can warm the feelings or inspire a devoted and sacrificial will.

Rudolf Steiner from early years made it his life's work to study and understand all the results of natural scientific investigations and to relate these to his ever widening experience of the realities of the spiritual world. He was then able to describe clearly in intellectual terms without any emotional suggestion or any sense of persuasion, the truths of the spiritual world. He says, over and over again, that it is not necessary for a person to become clairvoyant in order to test the truth of what he describes. The healthy human intelligence and sense of truth makes it possible to test what he says for oneself. Steiner also emphasised repeatedly that, to convey the truths of the spiritual world, one has to look at everything which needs to be understood from many points of view. To follow this kind of thinking is to make one's thinking alive.

This way of conveying the truth of the universe leaves the reader or listener entirely free. He comes through his own thinking to his own conclusions. He then discovers that, unlike the materialistic thinking prevalent today, his feeling life can respond to this new kind of thinking. He discovers too that he is no longer imprisoned by a deterministic inhuman will which shapes and organises so much of modern life, but his own individual will is stimulated to free conscious action. What he learns can raise enthusiasm and lead to practical deeds. In addition he learns from Steiner a path of inward development which can lead to the unfolding of new powers of spiritual perception. To nurture such a path of knowledge is the central task of the Anthroposophical movement, and the Society which serves it.

How is all this related to the practice and care of the sacraments in a church? I think the best way is to relate my own actual experience. I was brought up a Unitarian, and owe much to their wide, undogmatic approach to the culture of humanity. For the most part they regarded Jesus as a great human prophet. There was no conception of the incarnation, life, death and resurrection of the Logos of God.

My first approach to Anthroposophy was a scientific approach. Steiner's teaching about evolution, the four incarnations of the earth and the four kingdoms of nature threw light on the central problem of my youth, the relationship of science and religion. Here was something that must be studied further. I studied further, and before long I came to see without any kind of emotional conversion that the Mystery of Golgotha was not only the turning point in the evolution of man and of the earth, but the central key to unlock the meaning of the whole process. Through this event everything else becomes significant.

218

I gave up my profession and decided to become a minister. I had not yet met the Christian Community. The following year I experienced the Act of Consecration of Man for the first time. I cannot say that I 'understood' with my mind what took place. It was an immediate experience of a reality, the opening of doors and windows. I knew that this had to be my life's work. This does not mean that everyone who meets the sacraments has a similar experience. This simply illustrates the different kinds of contact with a spiritual reality.

I have already mentioned a kind of sharing of labour. Teachers, doctors, farmers, artists and many others have all found that their work can be inspired and renewed by Anthroposophy. So can the work of priests. We cannot all be our own doctors, teachers, farmers or artists, nor can we all celebrate our own baptisms, weddings or funerals. The new wisdom and the new impulse which flows through all the branches of Anthroposophical activity flows in a different way through the sacraments for all men. The approach is distinct, but as Rudolf Steiner himself said of the relationship of the two movements, they are not contradictory but complementary.

FURTHER READING

Alfred Heidenreich, *Growing Point. The Story of the Foundation of the Movement for Religious Renewal, The Christian Community* (Christian Community Press, 1965)

Evelyn Derry, *Seven Sacraments in the Christian Community* (Christian Community Press, 1966)

Christian Community Booklets
   The Act of Consecration of Man
   The Creed
   Marriage

Rudolf Frieling, *The Essence of Christianity* (Christian Community Press, 1971)

Rudolf Frieling, *The Metamorphosis of the Eucharist* (Christian Community Press)

Ormond Edwards, *A New Chronology of the Gospels* (Floris Books, 1974).

10. THE ANTHROPOSOPHICAL SOCIETY

by A. C. HARWOOD

Any new Movement needs a group of people to be its promoters and sustainers. The Roman orator, Cicero, once said 'If I had not my circle of hearers I would be unable to speak.' The initiate also must have his circle of hearers to whom he is able to speak, and Rudolf Steiner found his first circle in the German Section of the Anglo-Indian Theosophical Society. In 1912, however, he found himself in disagreement with that Society over a fundamental issue and he and most of the German members came out of it. These members—a very small circle—founded the first Anthroposophical Society, in which they became the hearers of the teaching of Anthroposophy and the bearers of the new impulse.

This first Society was indeed principally devoted to the 'hearing' of Anthroposophy, and its crowning achievement was the building of the first Goetheanum, a remarkable auditorium and stage, which could almost be described as a carving, and was the first example in the modern age of a building which united the arts of architecture, painting and sculpture. Rudolf Steiner once described it as 'the House of the Word'.

This society was a quite ordinary one of its kind though it may have been a little ahead of its time. Its Statutes even stated that it recognised no distinction of sex or religion—no small thing at that time. But it represented no new social impulse such as Steiner later wished to bring into the world. He himself acted as teacher to it but did not take part in its management. Indeed he was not even a member!

The first Goetheanum was burnt to the ground on New Year's Eve 1922/3. It was by then evident to Rudolf Steiner that there was an urgent need for a new Society with a new impulse. New types of members were joining the Society who found the old one formal and hierarchical, and who wanted to carry Anthroposophy into the world. Steiner, therefore, undertook the creation of a new Society at Christmas 1923.

He began by visiting a number of different countries where there were scattered groups of anthroposophists and encouraged them to form national—or, better said, territorial—Societies. Thus he visited England in September 1923, and as a consequence the Anthroposophical Society in Great Britain was then founded in his presence, and he agreed to become its President for life. But at the end of the year he brought together representatives of these newly founded territorial Societies, and many individual members as well, to a Foundation meeting of the new General Anthroposophical Society at Dornach, where the ruins of the old Goetheanum still remained. But he had conceived a totally different structure, the second Goetheanum, to take its place.

The new General, or World, Anthroposophical Society was to be an example of a truly modern Society. It may perhaps be said that its hall-marks were to be freedom, initiative and confidence. It was also to be a public Society, but one in which there would be a core of members seriously devoted to an esoteric path, who would be the real sustainers of the Anthroposophical Society and Movement. This new Society (henceforth called the Society) was not a federation of national Societies. The members joined it directly as individuals, and in the early days all membership cards were signed by Rudolf Steiner himself. It was expected that members in the different countries would join their territorial Societies, whose representatives also signed the membership card; but this was not obligatory, and any member was free to join the World Society alone, or even to become a member of another territorial Society.

The territorial Societies had an absolute right to form their constitutions and arrange their affairs in their own way, provided there was no conflict with the constitution of the World Society. Any seven individuals members could form a 'Group' for any purpose and on any basis they might choose.

It has been mentioned that Rudolf Steiner stood in the position of teacher to the earlier Anthroposophical Society which was administered—not always to his satisfaction—by a group of prominent members. This was entirely changed in the new Society. Rudolf Steiner himself became its President, uniting, as he said, his destiny with that of the Society. He proposed six collaborators—one of them, an English woman, died soon after—to work with him in the leadership of the Society, and they were all enthusiastically endorsed by the members at the Foundation Meeting. With Rudolf Steiner they formed the Executive or Vorstand (henceforth to be so called) of the Society.

What did all this mean? It meant that in future the impulse and content of Anthroposophy was no longer to be given from without but was to arise in the very centre of the Society. And where was it to arise? In an organ within the Society which Steiner called the School of Spiritual Science. This was the central core already referred to. There had been two aspects of Anthroposophy even in the old Society. First the presentation of a spiritual view of Universe, Earth and Man as perceived by the seer, and translated by him into the current language of ideas. Steiner always claimed that this 'anthroposophy' could be understood and accepted by the insight given to unprejudiced and healthy human reason, and should never be regarded or accepted as a dogmatic teaching. Secondly, there was instruction for those who wished to develop within themselves forces of higher knowledge, powers of cognition wider and deeper than those of the intellect. For the first, it was only necessary to join the Society, though even this form of knowledge made demands unusual in ordinary learned societies. The second, the deepening of experience described in such books as his 'Knowledge of the Higher Worlds—How is it achieved?' must now, he said, be sought for in the School of Spiritual Science.

The leadership of the School was vested in the 'Vorstand'. Any member of the Society could apply for admission to the School after two years membership of the Society—a period which enabled him to become acquainted with the basic elements of Anthroposophy. All members entering the School joined immediately the first class of the general Section which was 'to satisfy the needs common to man'. If a member worked in a particular branch of activity— education, medicine, science, art etcetera, he could apply for admission to a class designed to illuminate and inform any of these particular activities with esoteric knowledge and impulse.

To join the Society implied no obligation and no responsibilities on the part of the member. The obligation was only from the Society to him. It was open to everyone who considered the existence of such a thing as the Society and its institutions justifiable. Even those members could, and should, be admitted who were 'not very fitted for Anthroposophy'. To join the School was another matter. It implied a real responsibility in representing Anthroposophy before the world. It was a kind of free contract between the Vorstand and the member, the former providing the facilities of the School, and the latter undertaking not to develop any

initiative, or create any institution within the anthroposophical movement without prior consultation with the
Vorstand.

For although the Vorstand was described by Steiner as a
Vorstand of initiative and as such was a centre for the
whole anthroposophical movement, it was a centre far more
comparable to a heart than to a head. Blood flows to the
heart as well as from it, and initiative on the periphery
was as important to the Society as in the centre. But it was
obvious that such an initiative had to be brought into
harmony with that of the Vorstand itself and of other
members throughout the world. The constant flow of
communication between centre and periphery was something
Steiner considered of great importance. It was also exempli-
fied by his declaring that, when they were in Dornach, the
accredited leaders of the national Societies should sit with
the Vorstand at least as consultative members. The actual
members had naturally to reside in Dornach and be in
constant communication with each other.

It was obvious however that in the case of such a very
open Society the Vorstand could not undertake to work
with all members in the intimate manner which the School
required. The Vorstand had therefore the right to refuse
admission to the School to applicants they considered
unsuitable, and if members acted without consulting them
they could expect no cooperation from the School, from
which their action had virtually excluded them. Steiner
described it as a kind of imprisonment of the Vorstand if
they should be compelled to cooperate with those whom they
found unsuitable and intolerable.

In all this there appears the tremendous importance which
Steiner attached to building the Society on 'pure humanness'
and giving the greatest scope for the freedom and initiative
of the individual. Those members who expect to be
directed, who look to be told what to do, have joined the

wrong Society. This concrete 'humanness' becomes apparent in the whole structure of the School. At the Foundation meeting Steiner envisaged six sections, in addition to the general section to which everyone was to belong. Why six? Because there were six people with special qualifications and proved abilities to be the heads—or again shall we say the hearts—of these sections. They were the sections for Education, Art, Sculptural Art, Medicine, Science, and the Fine Arts. There would have been more Sections if there had been more suitable and proved people available. One, that for the plastic (sculptural) arts, was dropped with the death of Miss Maryon, who had been a close collaborator with Steiner in the carving in the first wooden Goetheanum, and who would have been responsible for this section.

In such ways the new Society was built on human beings, not on rules and regulations. Its Statutes, Steiner said, are not Statutes in the ordinary sense at all. They are descriptive of 'what is'.

The words 'human being' have, however, a wider connotation in Anthroposophy than prevails in the rest of the world. The so-called dead are 'human beings' in the spiritual world from where they give impulses to the living. Rudolf Steiner expected the members of the Society to act as in the presence of the dead, and to use every endeavour to extend their consciousness to that presence. Nor was this presence of spiritual beings to be confined to human beings in the spiritual world. The Protestant movement had finally jettisoned the Hierarchies. Nothing was to intervene between man on earth and the Almighty God. Steiner had restored the Hierarchies and described their place and functions. The work of the Society was to be undertaken as in their presence and with their help.

Steiner expected a great deal of his collaborators on the Vorstand. But he also laid on the members the responsibility of giving their complete trust and confidence to that Vorstand. Trust, he said, engenders strength for work in those to whom it is given. The understanding of Anthroposophy depends on insight, its administration depends on trust.

Thus for the first time in the world was created a truly public Society with a deeply esoteric core, not an elite core but a core to which every member might belong. But even those members who chose to belong to the Society alone were strongly urged by Steiner to meet together in groups. Anthroposophy may indeed be expressed in 'ideas' but those 'ideas' were won by the initiate out of the deep source of the heart and will, and they seek their source again in the one who hears them. Anthroposophy is a matter of the heart, rather than of the head; it is wisdom rather than knowledge. But it is here that man cannot live alone. He cannot live without someone to love, he cannot unfold his own will without the resistance or cooperation of other wills. You must learn, in a study group for instance, to appreciate even what you may consider dull and repetitive. You may know it already but it now comes to you from another soul. You may indeed learn in a group of things you did not know, but you go to the group because there are *people* there. Living ideas, unlike abstract concepts, are food for the soul, and can be experienced again and again, just as one eats the same physical food again and again.

This is indeed the answer to those who ask: Why should I join the Society when I can study the books for myself? You join in order to find the other person. Every time you find the other person you are in the spiritual world. The meeting of two friends—said the Greeks—is a god. You find that god most easily when you meet with others to study, to experience and to practise spiritual things.

There is a last matter to be added. Rudolf Steiner died hardly more than a year after he had formed the new Anthroposophical Society with its School of Spiritual Science. Much of what he intended had not yet been realised, and the members were left with fragments and indications only. Not all members understood his intentions. Others perhaps bungled in attempting more than they could achieve. There were acute differences of opinion, and for a time the Society was rent in two. But much has been learnt through these dissensions. There is a growing will to re-create the Society as a model Society of freedom, tolerance and initiative. The Society has been well described as 'an unfinished work of art'. It may in the long run prove to have been an advantage that the work was unfinished, because it calls on the will of the members to complete it. It is a challenge more especially to younger members to inspire and activate it, as the bearer of the spiritual impulse for the resurgence of man.

FURTHER READING

Rudolf Steiner, *The Life, Nature and Cultivation of Anthroposophy* (Anthroposophical Society in Great Britain, 1963)

Rudolf Steiner, *The Constitution of the School of Spiritual Science* (Anthroposophical Society in Great Britain, 1964)

Rudolf Steiner, *The Foundation Stone* (Anthroposophical Publishing Co. London, 1957)

F. W. Zeylmans van Emmichoven, *The Foundation Stone* (Rudolf Steiner Press, London, 1963)

FURTHER INFORMATION

The Anthroposophical Society in Great Britain and its local centres:
Rudolf Steiner House, 35 Park Road, London NW1 6XT.

Literature available:

Rudolf Steiner Press & Bookshop, 35 Park Road, London NW1 6XT

Rudolf Steiner Bookshop, 38 Museum Street, London WC1A 1LP

Anthroposophical Library, Rudolf Steiner House, 35 Park Road, London NW1 6XT

Rudolf Steiner Library, 38 Museum Street, London WC1A 1LP

Eurythmy and *Speech Formation*—courses, performances etcetera:

The London School of Eurythmy, Rudolf Steiner House, 35 Park Road, London NW1 6XT

The London School of Speech Formation, as above

Painting, Black and White Drawing classes:
Rudolf Steiner House, 35 Park Road, London NW1 6XT

Artistic Therapy—training course:
Artistic Therapy Centre, Fox Elms House, Tuffley, GLOUCESTER

Architecture:
The Architects' Group, c/o Emerson College, Pixton, FOREST ROW, Sussex

Education for normal children:

Steiner Schools Fellowship, c/o Emerson College, Pixton, FOREST ROW, Sussex

Curative Education

Rudolf Steiner Special Schools and Homes Information Centre, Claverley Cottage, Lubbock Road, CHISLEHURST, Kent BR7 5LA

Adult Education—details of courses and fields of study: Emerson College, Pixton, FOREST ROW, Sussex

Medicine:

Anthroposophical Medical Association, c/o Rudolf Steiner House, 35 Park Road, London NW1 6XT

Bio-Dynamic Agriculture:

The Bio-Dynamic Agricultural Association, Broome Farm, Clent, STOURBRIDGE, West Midlands

NPI:

NPI (International) 8 Valckenboschlaan, ZEIST, Holland; Pitchcombe House, Pitchcombe, STROUD, Glos.

The Christian Community—general information, addresses of local centres:

34 Glenilla Road, London NW3 4AP
Literature available: The Christian Community Press, 34 Glenilla Road, London NW3 4AP

The World Centre of The General Anthroposophical Society is at The Goetheanum, 4143 DORNACH, Switzerland. This can supply the addresses of National Societies, which in turn can give information on activities in their own countries.

THE CONTRIBUTORS

1. *John Davy* is Vice-Principal of Emerson College, an adult training centre based on the work of Rudolf Steiner.
2. *Cecil Harwood* was for many years a teacher at Michael Hall, and also Chairman of the Anthroposophical Society in Great Britain. He is Chairman of Rudolf Steiner Press and does much work for this and the London School of Eurythmy.
3. *Arne Klingborg* is a painter; Principal of the Rudolf Steiner Seminariet at Järna, Sweden, and Chairman of the Anthroposophical Society in Sweden.
4. *Rex Raab* is an architect, practising mainly in Germany.
5. *Eileen Hutchins* is a teacher at Elmfield School, Stourbridge.

   Thomas Weihs is Medical Consultant to the Camphill Rudolf Steiner Schools and the Camphill Village Trust.

   Francis Edmunds is a former teacher of Michael Hall School, and founder and Principal of Emerson College.
6. *Michael Evans* is a medical practitioner.
7. *Herbert Koepf* is Director of the School of Bio-Dynamic Farming and Gardening at Emerson College, and was formerly Professor of Soil Science in Heidenheim, Germany.

   Christopher Budd is a Director of the Budd-Thal-Jantzen partnership which distributes whole foods and provides a link between farmers and consumers.

8. *Christopher Schaefer* is a Director of the Centre for Social Development at Emerson College, and was previously teaching at the Massachussetts Institute of Technology, U.S.A.

9. *Oliver Mathews* is a priest of the Christian Community, He is one of the Lenkers for Great Britain.

10. *Cecil Harwood* see article 2.